The Concept of Human Rights in Africa

Issa G. Shivji

Professor of Law
University of Dar-es-Salaam
Tanzania

CODESRIA BOOK SERIES

The Concept of Human Rights in Africa

First published in 1989 by
CODESRIA BOOK SERIES
1 Ashdon Road, London NW10 4EH

CODESRIA is the Council for the Development of Economic and Social Research in Africa head-quartered in Senegal. It is an independent organisation whose principal objectives are facilitating research, promoting research-based publishing and creating multiple fora geared towards the exchange of views and information among African scholars. Its correspondence address is B.P. 3304, Dakar, Senegal.

ISBN 1 870784 02 2 (Paperback)
1 870784 03 0 (Hardback)

Production Consultants Foster & Phillips
Typeset by Emset, 1 Ashdon Road, London NW10 4EH
Printed by RyanPrint, 1 Ashdon Road, London NW10 4EH

The Concept of Human Rights in Africa

CONTENTS

ACKNOWLEDGEMENTS

I wrote this book in Harare, Zimbabwe during my sabbatical. Colleagues at the Faculty of Law, University of Zimbabwe provided the intellectual atmosphere which was very encouraging, enabling me to complete the task within a reasonably short period. I am grateful to Reg Austin and Ibbo Mandaza who took personal interest in facilitating my visit to, and stay in, Zimbabwe.

CODESRIA financed my visit to the Columbia Center for the Study of Human Rights in New York where I did all my library research. I am indebted to the Center's director Dr. Paul Martins for his friendly assistance. Ms. E. A. Widenmann, the African bibliographer of the Lehman's Library, put her enormous expertise on the location of the African material in the Library at my disposal. Without her help I would have taken much longer to locate relevant literature.

I am thankful to CODESRIA officers who facilitated my trip to New York. Their moral support was a great source of inspiration and personal pleasure. I am deeply aware that a word of thanks can hardly reciprocate their warmth and hospitality.

A number of friends read the manuscript in draft and made very useful comments. Wamba-dia-Wamba, Nick Amin, Jacques Depelchin, Reg Austin, Sheppard Nzombe and Mike Neocosmas took time off their busy schedules to discuss the manuscript with me. I am very grateful to them. Nick Amin spent long hours with me acting as a devil's advocate to help me sharpen some of the formulations and avoid inconsistencies in the manuscript. Wamba, in his usual incisive way, raised important issues all of which I may not have been able to integrate in the study. However, I used his observation on 'ideologies of domination/ideologies of resistance' to organise my thoughts in the Introduction.

Finally, my wife Parin was a strict disciplinarian and made me work through odd hours to see to it that the manuscript was completed without frivolous interruptions. To her I am ever indebted.

PREFACE

The Human Rights Discourse on and in Africa is intellectually backward, even by the standards of the African social science. That would not matter if it was also ideologically innocent. *That, it is not.* Human rights talk constitutes one of the main elements in the ideological armoury of imperialism. Yet from the point of view of the African people, human rights struggles constitute the stuff of their daily lives. For these two interconnected reasons, human rights talk needs to be subjected to a closer historical and political scrutiny.

Such a scrutiny cannot be politically neutral or intellectually uncommitted. The present work does not pretend to be so. Its point of departure and reference are the interests of the broad masses of the African people. In a sense, in the good sense of the word I hope, it is avowedly populist.

The Introduction, in broad strokes, looks at the state of struggles on the continent. I felt it was absolutely necessary to clarify the context within which I have approached the subject of human rights so as to avoid the pitfalls of a liberal perspective. Liberalism, including petty bourgeois radicalism, tends to absolutise the question of human rights as a central question and the rights struggle as the backbone of democratic struggles. It sees these issues as an end in themselves. As I explain and stress in the Introduction, the thrust of this study is fundamentally different.

Chapter One is mainly descriptive. It reviews the main debates of the dominant discourse. To give the reader a flavour of the debates and also to familiarise him/her with the terminology and the underlying concepts, I have let the discussants speak for themselves through copious quotations. Chapter Two is a critique. Admittedly, the critique does not dwell on details nor does it attempt to draw a balance sheet of the 'good' and the 'bad' in the discourse. Rather its aim is to lay bare the fundamental premises and the outlook that inform and direct the discourse. The chapter goes further and tries to elucidate the political and ideological consequences of such a discourse on the anti-imperialist, democratic struggles of the broad masses.

But the objective is not to throw away, so to speak, the human rights talk. The aim is to reconstruct the human rights ideology to legitimise and mobilise people's struggles. Chapter Three therefore threads together the main elements or the building blocks for a new perspective on human rights in Africa.

The three chapters clearly evince the fact that two tendencies in human rights discourse can be identified; the dominant tendency and, what I have called, the revolutionary tendency. The argument of Chapter Four is that the dominant tendency, taken to its logical conclusion, would end up with something like the *African Charter of Human and People's Rights.* The revolutionary tendency, on the other hand, finds expression (on that level) in the *Algiers Declaration of the Rights of Peoples.* Within their own paradigms, the two documents have serious limitations. For our purposes that is beside the point. The two documents are compared and contrasted in Chapter Four in the light of the critique of the dominant discourse and the proposed re-conceptualisation.

Originally this study had a very limited aim. Both CODESRIA (my sponsors) and myself were interested in formulating a concept paper on human rights in Africa with a view to formulate a research project. But as I dug into the existing literature, the subject became challenging (not because of its intellectual paucity but because of its ideologically and politically reactionary character) by the document resulting in this larger work.

Our hope is that this debate will dovetail, as it ought to, into the larger question of social movements and popular democratic struggles which have lately become the focus of intellectual work and academic research within some of the African research organisations.

Issa G. Shivji
Harare
August, 1988.

INTRODUCTION: RIGHTS IDEOLOGY AND RIGHTS STRUGGLE

IDEOLOGIES OF DOMINATION/IDEOLOGIES OF RESISTANCE

Once upon a time, in the continent's five centuries of domination and bleeding, 'black skins' were said to have no souls. They could be bartered for beads; gunned down like wild animals; packed like sardines; shipped like cattle and harnessed to a plough like horses without any compunction[1]. They had no souls, like mules. That was the ideology of domination. The transformation from a beast of burden to a labouring colonial native was a process of complex struggle producing not only slave revolts and heroes like Toussaint L'Ouverture[2] but also its own ideologies of resistance.

The colonial native had graduated. He probably had a soul but no brains. He was a child — a 'boy'[3]. He had no religion, no philosophy[4]. His soul had to be saved and his society to be civilised. And nothing could have more civilising effects than labour. Gunpowder, besides the bible, was used in abundance to reproduce the labouring colonial native. Labour he did, but so did he resist both the bible and the gun. Bows and arrows with a sprinkling of water[5] to protect against the gun were part of the ideology of resistance. So were the black churches in which the statue of Jesus was painted black[6]. Here then was an ideology of resistance reconstructed from the elements partly 'borrowed' from the ideology of domination but now turned on its head.

The transformation of the colonial native to an African 'moderniser' was again a complex process of struggle. Masses of 'natives' dipped into their torn pockets as they organised in trade unions and political parties; sending their representatives to the United Nations and sustaining themselves in a myriad of ways during strikes, boycotts, and lock-outs. The rituals, with their oath-taking ceremonies and divine sanctions, which the colonialist condemned as 'pagan', cemented camaraderie and solidarity of land armies whose heroism and guerilla tactics brought even the King's African Rifles almost to its knees[7].

Ideas come from practice, it is said: both ideas of domination and ideas of resistance. And the social clash between the dominated and the dominant produces even more ideologies of domination and of resistance. The colonial native of yesteryear, who had no history and was often the subject of the colonial anthropologist, now occupied the center-stage in the intellectual productions of the American political scientist, as an initiator, moderniser, nation-builder, investor and soldier. True, the ideology of 'modernisation'[8] had little staying power. The post-independence reality in Africa (and elsewhere) subverted these ideological constructs, refused to conform to ideal models and doggedly continued to produce ever newer forms of struggle and ideologies of resistance which defied text-book prescriptions. But those who produce text-books (intellectuals) have a professional interest in reproducing them. They believe it is ideas that produce things and practice should conform to their ideological prescriptions. Not surprisingly, until recently, little attention was paid, even by African producers of ideas, to the practice of struggle of their own people. In the intellectual scheme of things, the African intellectual slavishly parroted the Africanist guru, whether of the right or of the left. This intellectual domination was of course not a conspiracy of the intellect but a reflection of the continent's domination by imperialism.

Lenin said that there is no such thing as permanent peace among predators. Truces among imperialist powers are temporary, wars permanent. It is all a matter of that 'great' balance — the balance of forces. Witness the two wars within half a century; the fall of Pax-Britannica and the rise and the beginning of the fall of Pax-Americana. A generation of cold war involving intense 'spots of heat', all located on the three great continents, from Cuba to Vietnam and Algeria to Mozambique. While maintaining their cool in Europe and North America, the imperialists fought *wars* (by proxy) on our continents. The Third World became the hot-bed of resistance and revolutions generating its own ideologies of resistance. The cold war engendered the ideological picture of totalitarianism, sealed off behind the iron curtain, and the 'yellow peril' about to swallow up the 'white' free world. The crusade for democracy and human rights had begun.

The battlefield of that crusade though was not behind the iron curtain but on the rice-fields of the 'tri-continent'. The colonial native who had earlier been saved from anthropology and inserted in history was now to be tutored in democracy and human rights. His soul may have been saved from the paganist satan but his humanity had still to be protected from the totalitarian communist. Just as in the early

Christian crusades it was legitimate to save the soul even if it meant trampling the body, so in the human rights crusade it was fair to protect rights even while napalming the humans. 'Human rights ideology' is an ideology of domination and part of the imperialist world outlook. Like other ideologies of domination in yester-epochs, the dominant human rights ideology claims and proclaims universality, immortality and immutability while promulgating in practice class-parochialism, national oppression and 'patronising' authoritarianism. This work is all about this particular ideology of domination. But that is not all.

The dialectic between the dominated and the dominant operates on many different levels, ranging from actual social and national struggles to their theorisation, and from ideology to politics. Just as it is through class struggle that classes are historically constituted and politically demarcated, so in the realm of ideology, it is through a critique of the ideology of domination that the elements for the reconstruction of the ideology of resistance and struggle are crystallized. But this crystallisation is not dictated by an *a priori* logical plan which one has as a mental construct. Rather, it is a theoretical abstraction from life itself. Theory systematises what life produces confusedly. This study, seen from the vantage point of this Introduction, written later in time than the text, has been a kind of working out of that dialectic.

THE STUDY

Chapter One is a survey of the dominant discourse on 'human rights' in Africa. I have not spared on quotations from leading spokespersons of that discourse. The reader is entitled to the flavour and the taste of the prevailing debate. After all, as said earlier, human rights ideology is a very important component in the armoury of imperialist ideology to-day. That human rights ideology is part of an imperialist ideology is a conclusion of this study, not an assumption. It is through a close critique of the dominant discourse in Chapter Two that we arrive at this conclusion.

The critique, it is hoped, not only smashes the ideological edifice but challenges the intellectual coherence and consistency and the apparent solidity of the dominant human rights discourse. It is partly from the ruins of that edifice that the reconceptualisation offered in Chapter Three as an 'ideology of resistance' is constructed. This signifies a total ideological break with the dominant discourse. Continuity is only apparent but the break is real. A central task of the present study is in fact to develop an alternative ideological framework of 'human rights' as an ideology of resistance and an ideology of struggle of the large masses of Africa. But let it be said again that this ideological reconstruction is not a result of an intellectual process alone. I believe that the history and practice of struggles during the last three decades of independence in Africa have enabled us to attempt this theoretical systematisation. Even at the risk of being incomplete and sketchy, let me attempt to paint in broad strokes some aspects of that struggle.

THE STRUGGLE FOR DEMOCRACY AND THE PLACE OF RIGHTS-STRUGGLE

Three decades of independence on the African continent have witnessed a veritable accumulation of an unenviable track record: an average of maybe one-and-a-half military coups every year; an international debt which has mortgaged practically the labour-power of every man, woman and child on the continent for the rest of the next generation; the highest number of refugees in the world with half of the countries of the continent subsisting on starvation income. Meanwhile of course imperialism continues to leave large holes all over the continent as minerals are siphoned off and the soils exhausted from supplying commodities to satisfy the rapacious appetites of the industrial West.

Yet it was only a generation ago that the continent was ablaze with the fire of liberation after four centuries of abominable trading in slaves and a century of slavish trading in cocoa and coconuts.

Anti-colonial struggles, whether waged with guns as in Algeria and Mozambique, or negotiated at Lancaster House as in East Africa, was a mass political phenomenon. Politics then occupied the center-stage as masses took to the streets. Come political independence, however, and the actors on and off the stage swiftly changed costumes.

The new 'directors' cleared the stage of mass politics and the streets of the politics of the masses. Masses became mobs as strikes were re-christened riots. Colonial PCs (Provincial Commissioners) and DCs (District Commissioners) burnt their felt-hats and khaki stockings to don suits — even Kaunda and Nyerere suits — with brief-cases under their arms in place of sjamboks. Missionaries buried their rosaries and frocks to mount motor-bikes in jeans as they were re-consecrated as peace corps by 'archbishop' Kennedy. Banners of freedom, independence, justice and equality were repainted free trade, independent commerce and just and equal looting, this time under the guise of economic development.

The ideology of developmentalism, taking on different colours from Neo-Desturian socialism through Ujamaa to scientific socialism, was a thin veneer here and a thick fog there, all without exception masking the stark nakedness of underdevelopment and authoritarianism. But history in Africa has moved at a rapid pace, as has the suffering of its people. Some say it has come a full circle.

But the circle has not stopped at the same place where it started. Nay it is a spiral in motion. At this turn in the spiral, freedom, justice and democracy do not mean the same thing, even if the phrase is the same. The battle-cry of the day is for a second independence, not just independence. Even more significant, it is a battle-cry emanating from below and is not a constitutional creed preached from above.

The phrase 'democracy' falls pitifully short of describing this new struggle. But history has its own deceptive ways of hiding the new in the garb of the old. Even New Democracy or National Democracy is a temporary borrowing from other historical and cultural settings[9]. But the concept of a New Democratic Revolution as the present stage of the transformation in Africa better captures the objectives of the struggle.

Classical democracy is linked with the Western bourgeoisie which arose in Europe during the revolution that overthrew feudalism in, what have since been called, bourgeois democratic revolutions. The bourgeoisie marched apace and within a century transformed their countries of birth while marauding the rest of the world and planting its fangs all over the globe, including Africa. While unashamedly taking under its wings varied reactionary and backward social forces, from feudalists to zamindars and chiefs, in colonial countries, the imperialist bourgeoisie also gave rise to its own kind, although never nurtured it.

Simultaneously the penetration of monopoly capital stifled a full-blown development of a local bourgeoisie because of the need to keep the latter under its own domination. The local bourgeoisie, particularly in Africa, can hardly be said to have grown its own wings. It is compradorial[10] — a caricature of a bourgeoisie so well described by Frantz Fanon[11]. The African bourgeois democratic revolution was thus aborted.

Attempts at bourgeois democratic reforms in Africa, from Nigeria to Senegal, have not only been short-lived but almost farcical. Under the circumstances, the historic task of democracy, the task of constituting a civil society, falls squarely on the shoulders of the working people of Africa. That task can be fulfilled only in opposition to the state of the compradorial classes — the neo-colonial state[12]. For, by definition, the neo-colonial state has tended, for its own reproduction, to usurp and obliterate the autonomy of civil society and therefore the very foundation of democracy. It is within this formation that rights struggles, like other democratic struggles, have to be waged.

But these struggles are not and cannot be an end in themselves. Rather, these struggles must facilitate the constitution and crystallisation of the forces of a New Democratic Revolution. If so, democratic struggles from the standpoint of the popular classes of Africa ought to be new democratic struggles, i.e. democratic struggles with the perspective of a New Democratic Revolution[13]. The reconceptualisation of the 'human rights ideology' presented in this study is contextualised as an ideology of resistance and struggle within a New Democratic perspective.

No one can foretell the actual manifestations and forms of new democratic struggles. This will depend on each concrete situation. But we have already begun to see the upsurge of mass politics in Africa. South Africa is in that sense probably a dress-rehearsal of what is in store. Elsewhere too may be witnessed what has been called a 're-awakening of politics'[14]. The clarion call for democracy can be heard but that call is contradictory just as the bourgeois/liberal and the new democratic perspectives on democracy are contradictory. Similarly, the human rights ideology and the human rights-struggle manifest that contradiction. The task of this work is to demonstrate the contradictory perspectives on 'human rights'.

The forces of the New Democratic Revolution may be theoretically given — workers and peasants — but they have to be practically and politically constituted. The crystallisation of the motive forces of the New Democratic Revolution, I suggest, will be a long and a protracted process of struggles throwing up in its course varied ideologies of resistance. Dogmatism and demagogy about this process will only result in fruitless *putschism* and adventurism.

It is in this larger picture that we have attempted to locate the 'human rights ideology' and rights-struggle. In this we see the reconstituted 'rights ideology' at once as a critique of the imperialist 'human rights ideology' as at the same time an ideology of mobilisation and legitimisation of the struggles of the working people. Rights-struggles and rights-ideology may then be seen as components of new democratic struggles in the process of a New Democratic Revolution.

NOTES

1. A classic on slave trade remains Eric Williams, *Capitalism and Slavery*, London: Andre Deutch, 1964. See also Walter Rodney, *West Africa and the Atlantic Slave Trade*, Nairobi: East African Publishing House, 1967.
2. C. L. R. James, *The Black Jacobins*, London: Allison & Busby (revised edition), 1980.
3. On the colonial plantations of Tanganyika, African adult workers were 'boys'; African child workers were 'totos' (meaning children) and African female workers were 'bibis' (meaning mistresses).
4. Wamba-dia-Wamba has a good discussion of this ideology of domination which denied Africans philosophy and therefore capacity to think in his 'African

Intellectuals and Philosophy', paper read at the African Studies Association held at Denver, Colorado, USA, 19-23 November, 1987.

5. The famous resistance of the peasants of Tanganyika against the German imperialists in 1905 called the Maji Maji Uprising produced the ideology that bullets would rebound from the bodies sprinkled with water.
6. A number of African countries, including Kenya and Zaire, witnessed the rise of African church movement in which independent African churches were set up with deep anti-colonial ideology. In Kenya it was called Dini ya Musamba led by Elijah Masinde. (I am grateful to Shadrack Gutto for this information.)
7. The Mau Mau Uprising in Kenya in the '50s is an illustrative example.
8. For the various ideologies of domination produced on the morrow of independence see M.Mamdani, T.Mkandawire and Wamba-dia-Wamba, *Social Movements, Social Transformation and the Struggle for Democracy in Africa*, Working Paper 1/88, Dakar: Codesria, 1988.
9. Some elements of the concept are already present in Lenin's writings but only the Chinese experience and Mao's theorisation developed these into a full-blown theory. Revisionist Soviet writings have however totally vulgarised this concept by reducing it to describe neo-colonial states provided they have some 'progressive' international leanings including of course support for the Soviet Union. In Mao's conceptualisation, the New Democratic Revolution represents a transitional stage to socialism. The New Democratic State is a new state characterised by worker/peasant alliance with the leadership of the working class as opposed to the dictatorship of the proletariat which characterises a socialist state.
10. This is no place to develop fully the political economy of imperialist domination and class formations it engenders. I have argued elsewhere that imperialist invasion and subsequent domination sets into motion two tendencies in a dominated formation corresponding to its two-fold character i.e. monopolist and capitalist. Monopoly capital is in search of super-profits which is predicated on unequal exchange. The domination of the monopoly tendency stifles or thwarts the development of the capitalist tendency on a full scale. The social bearers of the imperialist tendency are the finance capital and the various local classes — feudalists, merchants, state bourgeoisie, settler landed classes etc. depending on the concrete social formation — with which it allies. These local classes I call compradorial. The capitalist tendency, on the other hand, is borne by the national bourgeoisie, which is a very weak formation in Africa if it exists at all, and various petty bourgeois sectors. The major producers of surplus are the workers and peasants who are subjected to super-exploitation, that is to say exploitation cuts into their necessary consumption thereby ensuring high rates of profit for monopoly capital. See generally my *Fight My Beloved Continent: New Democracy in Africa*, Harare: SAPES, 1988.
11. See Fanon's classical work *The Wretched of the Earth*.
12. Neo-colonialism is a social and political characterisation of a system of production which is dominated by monopoly capital or imperialism in alliance with local compradorial class/es and where exploitation of labour is predicated on the extraction of super-profits.
13. The New Democratic Revolution refers to profound class struggles combining both the national and social question; as a political revolution it means the 'smashing' of the neo-colonial state and setting up of a new democratic state characterised by a people's dictatorship under the leadership of the proletariat. As a social and economic revolution it means the transformation of the compradorial, imperialist-monopolist social relations of production into national, democratic relations - the concrete content of which of course depends on the nature and character of each formation. Proletarian leadership is to ensure that the National and Democratic

tasks are carried out thoroughly and consistently on the one hand, and to ensure movement towards socialism, on the other. See my *Fight My Beloved Continent* ... op.cit.

14. Issa G. Shivji, *Re-awakening of Politics in Africa*, public talk at the University of California, Berkeley, 1984.

1. THE DOMINANT DISCOURSE

INTRODUCTION

Human rights discourse has become one of the main 'growth points' of the academic industry in the last fifteen or so years. The output of literature on human rights in Africa has been enormous in quantity. To be sure, much of that literature has been of the expository kind, that is exposing human rights violations. Its academic character has been essentially journalistic while politically it has pretended to be neutral. Its philosophical assumptions, not unexpectedly, remain unsaid and implicit. However, in this work, I am not directly concerned with expository writings except probably to the extent that they reveal certain conceptual biases. But theoretical and conceptual writings on human rights in Africa, the direct subject-matter of this work, too have not been inconsiderable in volume.

If the volume of literature has been quite respectable, one cannot unfortunately say the same about its quality. Much of the literature tends to be repetitive of certain well-established issues and duplicate the same lines of argument or propaganda *ad infinitum.* Rather than review this literature religiously, an attempt will be made in the next sections to isolate the main trends and issues of the discourse.

This Chapter is concerned with what may be characterised as the dominant or prevailing discourse. This requires some explanation. By dominant here I mean the 'mainstream' of the debate. The mainstream has been constituted by that genre of academic and activist literature which has been routinely funded, been the subject of conferences, researched and published in the mainstream and widely circulated media including respectable publishing houses and scholarly journals, particularly in the West. There is, as always, a little sprinkling of peripheral literature which does not form part of the dominant discourse. It occasionally sees the light of day in the best of liberal tradition of token tolerance. There will be occasions at the appropriate places to refer to the latter type of literature as well.

Finally, the discourse discussed here comes mainly from what we call Africanists and Africans. Africanists are those in the developed

North — both activists as well as writers and scholars — concerned with human rights questions in Africa. Africans are African scholars and writers who write about human rights in Africa. I will have more to say about this so-called 'human rights community' in the relevant sections below.

UNIVERSALIZATION

This refers to the debate on whether, and to what extent, human rights conceptions are universal or culturally relative. The arguments usually proceed from the various international, particularly United Nations, instruments on human rights which declare their content to be universal. The parent instrument in this regard is of course the *Universal Declaration of Human Rights* of 1948.

The discourse itself is fairly confused and shot with expectedly all kinds of primordial prejudices which more often than not remain unacknowledged. The arguments are made at different levels although these levels are rarely distinguished in the literature. Four levels may be isolated for the purposes of exposition here.

The first level relates to the historical genesis and philosophical basis of human rights. Apparently there is a fair degree of consensus that human rights conceptions embodied in the various instruments are of Western origin. Further that even their conceptual framework and philosophical basis have their roots in the specific circumstances of the Western society. While there is a considerable amount of consensus on the historical genesis of human rights[1], there is not as much agreement as to the roots of its philosophical basis. Many African and Third World writers[2] have argued that the philosophy and conceptions of human rights existed in other cultures as well[3] although some of the Western conceptions may not have parallels in the traditional conceptions of human rights in Africa.

On the other hand, the counter-claimers on this score have argued forcefully that human rights conceptions *per se* simply did not exist in the pre-colonial African societies. What are usually put forward as African human rights conceptions by its proponents are nothing more than notions of human dignity and worth which existed in all societies. One of the strongest proponents of this line puts it thus:

> There is no specifically African concept of human rights. The argument for such concept is based on a philosophical confusion of human dignity with human rights, and on an inadequate understanding of structural organization and social changes in African society. Underlying this

> inadequate understanding, a number of assumptions regarding the meaning of culture are used to buttress the reliance on the assertion of 'cultural relativity', in order to argue that the allegedly 'Western' concept of human rights cannot be applied to Africa[4].

The next level of argument relates to the validity and applicability of human rights conceptions. Do they have universal validity and applicability even though they may have originated in the West? Howard[5] and Donnelly[6] answer this with a definite 'yes'. Although they originated in the West and have a philosophical basis there, human rights conceptions have universal validity and applicability in Africa as elsewhere.

Human rights as defined by Howard are understood as individual claims or entitlements against the state and in this sense there is only one conception of human rights and that is Western. As many of the African countries have undergone the modernization or individuation process together with the rise of states, this conception applies and ought to apply to them as well. Kannyo, in an analysis which puts greater weight on the rise of the state in colonial Africa, arrives at a similar conclusion although through a different route.

> To the extent that the Western model of the state has spread to other parts of the world, the factors which gave rise to the need for constitutional guarantees and led to the evolution of the philosophy of human rights in the West have become equally relevant in other parts of the world. Moreover, the core elements of the concept of human rights are not alien to non-western cultures. Traditionally, most of the cultures have given the greatest importance to the preservation of life and the promotion of human welfare[7].

The position of many Western-trained African jurists is also entrenched within the liberal thought although less sophisticated than that of African social scientists. Asante's assertion on this score may be taken as representative of that position.

> I reject the notion that human rights concepts are peculiarly or even essentially bourgeois or Western, and without relevance to Africans. Such a notion confuses the articulation of the theoretical foundations of Western concepts of human rights with the ultimate objective of any philosophy of human rights. Human rights, quite

> simply, are concerned with asserting and protecting human dignity, and they are ultimately based on a regard for the intrinsic worth of the individual. This is an eternal and universal phenomenon, and is as vital to Nigerians and Malays as to Englishmen and Americans[8].

The proponents of cultural-specificity, on the contrary, argue that human rights as conceived in the West are rejected in the Third World and Africa precisely because their philosophical basis is not only different but indeed opposite. Whereas Western conceptions are based on the autonomous individual, African conceptions do not know such individualism. In traditional Africa, the human being found his (sic!) worth within the community to which he related in terms of obligations and duties[9].

> Whatever the diversity among third world countries in their traditional belief systems, individuals still perceive themselves in terms of their group identity. Who and what an individual is has been conceptualized in terms of the kinship system, the clan, the tribe, the village, whatever the specific cultural manifestations of the underlying prevailing world view[10].

This argument has met with a forceful rebuttal from both the left-liberal and conservative Africanists. The left-liberal, probably most strongly represented in the writings of Rhoda Howard, have gone even further and discovered a conspiracy by the ruling class in this line of argument. They have argued that African societies have undergone fundamental transformations in the direction of individualisation since colonialism. The picture of a traditional communitarian society is in fact a non-existent idyll painted by African rulers from Kaunda to Nyerere to hide and rationalise their own unbridled violations of human rights. To use her own language:

> ...Some African intellectuals persist in presenting the communal model of social organization in Africa as if it were fact, and in maintaining that the group-oriented, consensual, and redistributive value system is the only value system and hence that it ought to be the basis of a uniquely African model of human rights. Ideological denials of economic and political inequalities assist members of the African ruling class to stay in power[11].

The third level of argument proceeds to identify and catalogue rights in traditional African society which are said to be similar to those found in the West or in the modern conceptions of human rights. Keba M'Baye[12] and Dunstan Wai[13], among others, have been associated with this type of approach. 'In any event', says M'Baye, 'pre-colonial Africa possessed a fitting system of rights and freedoms, although there was neither the recognition nor the clear formulation of such rights and freedoms as they are recognized, formulated and analyzed today'[14].

Eze has taken issue with this type of, what he calls, 'romanticism'. Eze argues that M'Baye is confusing the humanism and socialism of 'primitive societies' with the so-called modern, or bourgeois, conceptions of human rights. He argues that the whole question of rights is dependent on the stage of development of a particular society. Eze says that it is erroneous to say that the catalogue of rights mentioned by M'Baye was invariably and at all times respected in the traditional African society. That in Africa too, with the development of feudalism, the so-called rights were eroded and that organised derogations of human rights — for example, slavery, inferiority of women etc. — were not unknown. However, unlike Howard, Eze seems to believe that Africa did have conceptions of human rights *qua* rights but cautions that the degree of their protection has to be concretely examined[15].

The fourth and final level of argument has been to locate human rights specifically within a cultural-relativist paradigm. This argument proceeds typically by asserting that African societies had conceptions of human rights which differed from the Western and that indeed Western societies may do well to learn from some of these specifically African conceptions.

The usual emphasis in this regard is on the communal nature of rights; social harmony and emphasis on obligations and duty to the community, etc. Cobbah[16] has criticised the Eurocentric views and perspectives on human rights and argued for an Afrocentric perspective. As a matter of fact, he says, there should be cross-cultural understanding which would add and contribute to the development of international human rights norms. He summarises his argument as follows:

> I have attempted to point out that Africans do not espouse a philosophy of human dignity that is derived from a natural rights and individualistic framework. African societies function within a communal structure whereby a person's dignity and honour flow from his or her transcendental role as a cultural being. Within a changing world, we can expect that some specific aspects of African

> lifestyles will change. It can be shown, however, that basic Afrocentric core values still remain and that these values should be admitted into the international debate on human rights. The debate I believe should be on whether these cultural values provide human beings with human dignity. We should pose the problem in this light, rather than assuming an inevitable progression of non-Westerners toward Western lifestyles. If we do this then we can really begin to formulate authentic international human rights norms[17].

Fasil Nahum argues in a similar vein. Africa, he says, has its humanity to contribute to the rest of the world. Under African humanism, he asserts, the individual is not dissected into an economic man divorced from his other characteristics but is taken as a whole and is taken within his community. In other words, individual rights are not emphasised, or rather over-emphasised, at the expense of collective rights. Nahum therefore sees the principle of 'comprehensiveness' and 'harmony' which can be contributed by Africa to the international norms of human rights[18].

And finally, Al-Na'im brings the Islamic standpoint to bear on the cultural relativist position. He argues that Islam cannot be totally discarded on the question of human rights. Partly for tactical reasons but partly also because people understand things through their cultural artifacts, the whole question of human rights too has to be viewed through Islamic lenses in Muslim African countries. But there are aspects of Islam and the Shari'ah law which cannot be accepted in the modern world. And Islamic countries themselves, by accepting international covenants, have accepted the universality of human rights. These have to be integrated with Islamic positions. This can be done without sacrificing Shari'ah as a whole but by modifying it in the true spirit of Islam. This is how he puts it:

> The international human rights movement has succeeded in establishing universal human rights standards for religious minorities based on moral as well as pragmatic arguments. Faced with these arguments, modern Muslim countries have had to participate in the formulation and adoption of the standards, not only at the international level, but also at the regional and national levels. Nevertheless, extremely serious tensions exist between these standards and the Muslims cannot and should not be allowed to justify discrimination against and persecution of non-Muslims on the basis of Islamic cultural norms.

> The Muslims themselves must seek ways of reconciling Shari'ah with fundamental human rights. The choice of the particular methodology for achieving these results must be left to the discretion of the Muslims themselves. A cultural relativist position on this aspect of the problem is, in my view, valid and acceptable. I should argue, however, that no cultural relativist argument may be allowed to justify derogation from the basic obligation to uphold and protect the full human rights of religious minorities, within the Islamic or any other cultural context[19].

The latter argument would probably be accepted even by Howard and Donnelly — the argument of what has been called weak cultural relativism[20]. Other Western liberals[21] have also gone along with the earlier arguments about African perspectives making contribution to international human rights. Typically, though, they pay lip service to African contribution without substantially modifying their own Western positions and perspectives. The Butare Colloquium on Human Rights and Economic Development in Francophone Africa probably summarised the consensus on this issue quite well.

> The colloquium agreed that, for many reasons, the automatic adoption of traditional rights, even if that were possible, would be inappropriate. The more important status given to the individual vis-a-vis the group in modern society was cited as one constraint; also, the traditional hierarchical structure which characterized most pre-colonial societies has largely disappeared. It therefore becomes necessary to select among the traditional rights and to determine how the positive values of traditional society can best be translated into modern African reality[22].

THEORISATION

A note

The survey of human rights literature on Africa reveals one significant gap. There is very little written by Africanists, and even less by Africans themselves, on the philosophical and conceptual foundations of human rights in Africa. In other words, one can hardly talk of the

African philosophy of human rights, using that concept as developed by Paulin Hountondji[23]. What exists is simply African ethno-philosophy of human rights which has been covered in the preceding section. The philosophical discussion therefore which may have certain relevance to Africa is largely Western and its Marxist critique originating mainly from the Soviet Union and East European countries. As for conceptual/theoretical foundations of human rights, the discussion has been dominated largely by African lawyers and confined to positivist legal questions without much discourse on their jurisprudence. This absence and biases will be reflected as we discuss the conceptual foundations of human rights in Africa in subsequent sections.

Human rights on moral and legal planes

THE MORAL PLANE

The philosophical discussion on human rights broadly divides into two major tendencies: that which relates to some form of natural law theory and that which subscribes to positivism. Natural law, traced from ancient Greece through the medieval period and Enlightenment to its post-world war II revival, is considered to be the parent of natural rights[24]. Natural rights therefore trace their origin and claim legitimacy from a certain moral/ethical (including religious during the medieval period) world view.

All the Western/European great declarations of rights from the *English Petition of Rights* (1627) through the *American Declaration of Independence* (1776) to the French *Declaration of Rights of Man and Citizen* (1789), are said to be within this natural law tradition. It is within this same tradition that the philosophers of the seventeenth and eighteenth centuries developed their rights-theories. Among these the most-quoted are of course John Locke, Thomas Hobbes and Rousseau. Modern conceptions of human rights in the West in fact draw their inspiration directly or indirectly from the writings of these philosophers.

In the hands of the seventeenth and eighteenth century philosophers, the natural law tradition and its concomitant natural rights theories translated themselves into political liberalism whose center-piece is the theory of individualism. In Hobbes, Locke and Rousseau the autonomous individual in pursuit of his survival and happiness enters into the erstwhile social contract now to escape from the brutish nature to establish order (Hobbes), or to install a limited government (Locke) or, as in Rousseau, to constitute the General Will without, in any case, divesting himself of his natural rights. Indeed, by now the ubiquitous individual is the sole possessor of natural rights of life, liberty and property; a free, autonomous contractarian.

But there was a century-long interlude in this tradition when positivism rose high during the second half of the 19th and the first half of the 20th centuries. The positivist pundits mercilessly tore down the natural law tradition and considered the idea of natural rights a 'nonsense on stilts'[25]. Auguste Comte, who is considered the founding father of positivism, in so many words declared 'natural rights' and 'rights of man' as a set of beliefs or ideology about reality supporting the self-image of the rising middle classes[26]. The 20th century positivists like Hans Kelsen took positivism to its most abstract logical form where rights almost disappeared and what remained were simply obligations ultimately traceable to the fictitious grundnorm — fictitious in Kelsen's theory but as real as the state can be, in practice[27].

Nazism gave positivism a rude shock when under state-ordained laws massive atrocities were committed. Natural law and natural rights, by this time under the name of human rights, were resurrected as even positivists like Hart and Fuller wrangled to provide their 'positivism' with a minimum natural law content[28]. It was in the same vein of the revival of natural law that the language of natural rights penetrated the early UN Declarations. The natural law and natural rights concepts of the early philosophers have penetrated even the modern and, in the West, the most fashionable works of Dworkin[29] and Rawls[30].

Major critiques of these conceptions of human rights have come from Marxist writers, particularly from the Soviet bloc. The critique has revolved mainly around the failure to situate human rights conceptions historically and socially. Natural law, and even positivist conceptions of human rights arose at certain historical periods and represented the interests of definite classes. Therefore there is no such thing as human rights conceptions which are eternal and true for all times. As one Professor from the German Democratic Republic puts it:

> Human rights are neither eternal truths nor supreme values ...They are not valid everywhere nor for an unlimited time. They are rooted neither in the conscience of the individual nor in a God's plan of creation. They are of earthly origin ... a comparatively late product of the history of human society — and their implementation does not lie in everybody's interest. In their essentials, man's interest are not the same everywhere and they cannot even be the same in any particular country under the conditions of the system of private ownership of the means of production[31].

The 'socialist' critique then proceeds to argue that human rights at the national level are exclusively those provided in the positive law and therefore granted by the state. On the international level, on the other hand, there are two types of human 'rights'. There are those which are to be found in Declarations which are only claims or aspirations and those which are in the binding covenants and treaties i.e. in the positive international law[32].

In short, the 'socialist' critique has emphasised the ideological nature of human rights generally, and particularly the so-called natural rights, as at the same time argued to locate them specifically within the existing socio-economic context.

As it was said earlier, this short discourse on the philosophical foundations of human rights has been essentially among the scholars of the North and there has been very little contribution from Africans. Eze in his book-length study of human rights closely follows the 'socialist' critique while other African writers in their review of philosophical foundations follow the usual Western line.

THE LEGAL PLANE

Among Western philosophers of human rights there has been some discussion as to the distinctive or otherwise character of 'rights' on moral and legal planes[33], but this need not detain us. As for Africanists and Africans, the discussion has been set squarely on the legal plane. This has been on two levels, national and international.

The national has pertained to the nature of the constitutions in Africa, the extent to which they do or do not protect human rights and, even if they do, how far these are respected and enforced. These debates have been much more within specific country[34] studies rather than continental or comparative works[35]. On the international plane, the debate has taken the UN instruments (now collectively called the International Bill of Rights) as their point of departure, and generally argued on the relevance or lack thereof of these to Africa, the mechanisms for their protection and the desirability of regional system of protection of human rights[36]. Here we briefly chart the main bones of contention on these two levels that have dominated the discourse in so far as they are relevant to conceptual issues.

Most black African countries, as they marched into independence in the '60s, were bequeathed the Westminster constitutional and political order in the former British colonies, while constitutions in French-speaking Africa were modelled on analogies taken from France or Belgium. In both cases, in their human rights provisions, the models departed from those found in the mother countries. Britain of course does not have a written constitution and follows the principle of the sovereignty of the parliament. There the protection of human rights, it is said, is based on constitutional conventions and traditions.

Yet all the former British colonies were given written constitutions with the protection of fundamental rights as part of the independence package. The French independence constitutions paid homage to human rights usually modelled on the International and European Conventions, although following the French practice, these were not reviewable by independent institutions such as courts[37].

It has been argued by many writers that the motive behind the inclusion of fundamental rights in the independence constitutions was to protect the property interests of the settler minority and foreign companies with investments in the former colonial economies. This argument is buttressed by the fact that the same powers were little concerned with fundamental rights, separation of powers, or independent judiciary etc. during their own rule in the colonies. One group of lawyers has argued thus:

> In the late fifties and early sixties when the colonies were nearing independence the issue of Bill of Rights came to the fore. It was raised by the very powers that had been suppressing it for years. But this time there was a good reason for it. The colonisers were leaving. The colonised were ascending into power. What of the property accrued during the whole period of colonialism by the nationals and companies of the colonial powers? This had to be protected. Therefore the issue of the individual rights, especially the rights to own private property and state protection of the same, became one of the main topics of discussion on independence. In the now notorious Lancaster House constitutional talks, the British made sure that a Bill of Rights was entrenched in the constitutions of its former colonies. Not that they cared a lot about individual rights and freedoms of the indigenous people. They were concerned about the property of their nationals still in the colonies after independence[38].

This, to be sure, has been a minority strand of argument. And it has developed into two contradictory directions. In one view, it is used to rationalise the absence of both the provisions for, and particularly the practice of, human rights protection where the so-called tradition and authenticity are counter-weighed against 'colonial' conceptions of freedoms and rights[39].

In the other view, it is argued that while 'rights-protection' is extremely important and should find a place in African constitutions, this cannot take the same form or show the same concerns as in metropolitan countries[40]. The dominant argument, however, propounded by most of the African and Africanist lawyers and jurists, has proceeded on the basis of an uncritical acceptance of Western liberal conceptions of what is called 'constitutionalism' and the rule of law[41]. Since this conceptualisation is well-known and the African legal discourse has added little to it that is new, it need not detain us further.

On the international plane, the activity of the African and Africanist jurists has been, almost exclusively, to develop a regional mechanism of 'human rights' protection and adoption of an African Convention of Human Rights[42]. The discourse has therefore revolved around some comparative understanding of the European and Inter-American models. Since the adoption of the African Charter, a largely legal analysis of the Charter, which I will discuss at the appropriate place below (see Chapter.4) in some detail, has ensued.

'Human' and 'rights' in human rights

Natural law once again provides the point of departure in the definition of 'human' in human rights so far as the Western liberal theories are concerned. In the Lockeian and Hobbesian schema 'human nature' is posited *a priori*, pre-existing any form of political organisation. Various qualities and characteristics including 'rights' then pertain to this 'human' and constitute his essential 'nature'.

In this sense these rights are said to be 'inalienable', 'imprescriptible' or 'inherent'. Modern natural lawyers would probably not make their positions so explicitly supernatural although they too assume certain 'original' conditions which come very close to the natural law framework[43]. Natural rights, then, being part of the very nature of a human being, attach to all human beings everywhere and in all societies. 'His "natural" rights attach, by virtue of his reason, to every man much as do his arms and legs. He carries them about with him from one society to another. He cannot lose them without losing himself'[44]. Not only natural rights attach and are part of human nature but they are discovered by reason — another *conditio specifica* of being human and a specific contribution of the rationalists to the natural law theory.

Rights are simply moral and legal claims and/or entitlements. The distinction between the 'moral' and the 'legal' is that between 'ought' and 'is'[45]. Legal human rights *are* those that are to be found in the positive law while moral human rights are claims which *ought* to be in the positive law. In its modern form, where the dominant terminology has taken the phrase 'human' rather than 'natural' rights, human right is defined as a 'universal moral right, something which all men, everywhere, at all times ought to have, and something of which no one may be deprived without grave affront to justice, something which is owing to every human being simply because he is human'[46]. African writers, particularly jurists, even if implicitly, accept this definition.

In an otherwise socialist approach, surprisingly Eze's definition comes close to the one just quoted. Eze defines human rights as: 'Human rights represent demands or claims which individuals or groups make on society, some of which are protected by law and have become part of ex lata while others remain aspirations to be attained in the future'[47].

The other approach has been to argue that the conception of rights is strictly a legal concept and there is no such thing as extra-legal or moral rights. Indeed the rights-talk on the moral plane is an extension of rights-concepts from the legal plane. Andrew Levin explains.

> Right is, by origin, a legal concept that, since the seventeenth century, has figured prominently throughout moral discourse. In its original sense, a right is a claim advanced by an individual or group, enforceable by law... To talk of rights is to talk of what the law ought to enforce, not of what it does in fact enforce... And so, very early on, the concept of right outgrew its strictly legal sense. By right, then, is understood any legitimate claim advanced by an individual or group[48].

For Rhoda Howard there is only one universal conception and formulation of human rights. Human rights are universal. 'They inhere in human beings by virtue of their humanity alone'[49]. Furthermore they are neither privileges nor contingent upon any duties but entitlements against the state[50]. Edward Kannyo, perhaps less forcefully, also takes a similar position in relating both the origin and the existence of rights as against the state[51].

The 'socialist' critique takes a strictly positivist view. While it does not accept any notion of an eternal human nature abstracted from historical and social conditions, it argues that there is no such concept as 'rights' outside state-law. And the so-called 'natural rights' are not rights at all but some kind of moral ideals. '...The human rights embodied in natural law are neither laws nor rights, but moral ideals, or shall we say: pretensions conceived of as rights, formulated in respect of the law-to-be-created; accordingly, they should not be called rights at all'[52].

Finally, those who challenge the universality of the Western concepts and argue for an Afrocentric conception of human rights, take the position that the African traditional conception does not know of a human being outside his community and culture. 'I am because we are, and because we are therefore I am', is a summing up of the African philosophy of existence, according to Cobbah[53]. This perspective emphasises that the traditional African society is based on 'obligations' rather than rights; not obligations or duties conceived as correlates of rights (as in Hohfeld) but obligations as the organising principle of kinship and family relationships[54].

As for the cataloguing and classification of rights, the discourse is fairly non-controversial. One can say that there are two major forms of classification. The first is in terms of what is called the traditional classification between 'political/civil' rights and 'social and economic' rights. The other classification is in terms of three 'generations' of rights.

Eze groups various rights under five headings: civil, political, social, economic and cultural. Civil and political rights include the right to self-determination; the right to life; freedom from torture and inhuman treatment; freedom from slavery and forced labour; the right to liberty and security; freedom of movement and choice of residence; the right to a fair trial; the right to privacy; freedom of thought, conscience and religion; freedom of opinion and expression; the right of assembly; freedom of association; the right to marry and found a family; the right to participate in one's government either directly or through freely elected representatives; and the right to nationality and equality before the law. Economic, social and cultural rights embrace *inter alia* the right to work; the right to just conditions of work; the right to fair remuneration; the right to an adequate standard of living; the right to organise, form and join trade unions; the right to collective bargaining; the right to equal pay for equal work; the right to social security; the right to property; the right to education; the right to participate in cultural life and to enjoy the benefits of scientific progress[55].

Welch relates the three generations of rights to the role of the state therein thus:

> The first generation stressed civil and political rights, notably liberty against governmental intrusions on individuals. The second generation emphasized economic, social and cultural rights, by which equality rather than liberty was the watchword, and for which governments were to pursue collective achievement of betterment. Third generation rights, by contrast, involve solidarity, both among developing states as a group, and among all states in general[56].

Kibola, on the other hand, has pointed out that it is not so much the question of generation of rights in some abstract form but rather that these group of rights reflect specific historical stages and demands of social groups at a particular stage. The first generation of rights, with its emphasis on liberty and equality, was essentially representing the interests of the rising bourgeoisie against the feudal bondage; the second generation of rights represents the coming on stage of socialism with its accent on social and economic equality while the third generation rights 'have emerged out of the plight of the third world countries which have been exploited for many decades'[57].

Holders of rights: individuals, states, people

The Western liberal thought firmly holds that rights attach to individuals; individuals constitute both the unit of organised society as well as the primary holders of rights. The autonomous individual, in the liberal theory, exists anterior to organised society and comes into it with his rights even if not totally intact but voluntarily surrendered, in part, through a social contract. This traditional view, as we have seen, has been severely attacked by socialist critics.

The latter, in their strict positivist approach, would argue that within domestic jurisdictions it is the citizens who are the holders of rights 'given' them by respective laws. These rights are not the result of any whimsical benevolence of the state but a result of, or a compromise in, the struggle of social forces which may objectively find expression in the laws of the land, notwithstanding that these laws ultimately reflect the will of the ruling class[58].

On the international plane, the subject of the traditional international law, the state, is also the subject of rights, according to the 'socialist' position which all along the line strictly upholds state sovereignty. Presumably then such rights as 'right of people to self-determination' are exercisable only through the agency of states (except in a colonial or colonial-type situation)[59].

Although premised on a culturalist standpoint, many African writers come close to the 'socialist' position. The argument here emphasises, once again, that African traditional society is based on a collectivity (community) rather than on an individual. And therefore the notion of individual rights is foreign to African ethnophilosophy. On the international plane, on the other hand, while the African state position has vigorously argued for collective rights such as 'right of people to self-determination', they would still assert that the state is the primary subject of international law and therefore it is only through the state that rights (including rights of people) can be exercised[60].

The debate has concretely found expression in the discussion of the international covenants, particularly the *International Covenant on Economic, Social and Cultural Rights,* 1966 and the *International Covenant on Civil and Political Rights,* 1966[61]. Article 1(1) of both these Covenants, in identical phraseology, stipulates that 'All peoples have the right to self-determination. By virtue of that right they freely determine their political status and freely pursue their economic, social and cultural development'. This, among other things, has led many leading international lawyers to argue that collectivities as holders of rights are recognised by international law[62]. There are still those who would hold that this particular 'right' is not a right at all but simply a principle. 'Thus fundamental rights were not those of groups but of the individuals'[63].

The position of the African ethnophilosophy on the communitarian nature of the traditional African society was made a cornerstone of the African Charter on Human and People's Rights (see below ch.4) which stipulates certain rights as being the rights of the people. In this debate between individual and group or collective rights, some Africanists have taken a firm position that 'the individual as individual is the basic unit of human rights. The stress on 'group' rights in the African Charter of Human and People's Rights simply derogates from individual rights in favour of the 'rights' of nation-states or, ..., in favour of the 'rights' of their ruling classes'[64]. The dominant Africanist position, though, seems to be the one summed-up by Elston and Eide in the following fashion:

> Commonly, individuals have been considered the subjects. This does not any longer fully capture the normative reality: by the covenants on human rights adopted by the United Nations in 1966, peoples obtained the right of self-determination. Thus, also collectivities can be subjects of human rights[65].

Responsibility and sanctions

The next conceptual question which arises perpetually, particularly among international lawyers, is: who is responsible for these rights? In other words, where does the duty to respect these rights lie? And by the same token what sanctions, if any, apply when these rights are breached or violated?

The answers to these questions have been as clear as those which place the obligations squarely on the states to those which amorphously refer to the 'international community' as organised in the United

Nations. It is said that states or governments, who constitute the ultimate organised authority in society, are responsible not to interfere with the freedoms and rights of individuals (negative obligations) as well as effect and help to realise certain rights such as economic and social/cultural rights (positive duties).

Even more problematic have been collective rights. One answer, in the context of the right to self-determination, has been, to quote once again Alston and Eide:

> On the one hand, the people concerned has a duty to strive for self-determination, and the government which controls that people, be it a colonial government, an occupant, or a government which does not include representatives of the people concerned — that government has an obligation to accept and promote self-determination for the people concerned. But beyond this, the international community, as organized by the United Nations, also has a responsibility to assist the people in its struggle for self-determination and also to oppose the continued oppression by the colonial, occupying or non-representative government[66].

The other, even more controversial and relatively unsolved problem, relates to the question of sanctions against the violators of human rights[67]. The present debate revolves around the traditional positivist view, which happens to be also the traditional 'socialist' view, that ultimately it is the state within the boundaries of particular countries which have legitimate jurisdiction to redress breaches and violations of human rights. This view thus upholds state sovereignty and finds favour with African states.

The other view argues for some inter-state system, either the United Nations, or a regional body, which would be responsible — ultimately even for the use of force — to punish infractions of human rights. The usual model here is the inter-European system as crystallized in the European Convention on Human Rights[68] and the provisions of the UN Charter on the use of force, which presumably it seeks to generalise. Finally, there are peripheral views which emphasise the importance of publicity and exposure by non-governmental organisations as a possible sanction against violations of human rights.

PRIORITIZATION

Political/civil *vs* social/economic rights

Political and civil rights are considered the classical or the first generation rights firmly embedded within the Western liberal tradition. These emphasise equality and liberty of the individual in law and morality, including the freedom and liberty to pursue equally property or poverty. Social and economic rights, on the other hand, are considered the second generation rights and associated with the rise of socialism and particularly the victory of the Bolshevik Revolution in Russia in 1917. Socialists give priority to social and economic equality and consider these the bed-rock of other superstructural rights which, they argue, simply benefit the propertied few in absence of social/economic rights[69].

African scholars and politicians not only stress the priority of social and economic rights but also seek to justify curtailment of civil and political rights, as traditionally understood, in the interest of economic development. The argument is often expressed in such rhetorical questions as:'How can a peasant from the bush appreciate freedom of expression, when the possibility of having modern fertilizers at his disposal would be much more valuable for him?'[70]. One of the most articulate, and relatively democratic, African leaders puts it thus:

> What freedom has our subsistence farmer? He scratches a bare living from the soil provided the rains do not fail; his children work at his side without schooling, medical care, or even good feeding. Certainly he has freedom to vote and to speak as he wishes. But these freedoms are much less real to him than his freedom to be exploited. Only as his poverty is reduced will his existing political freedom become properly meaningful and his right to human dignity become a fact of human dignity[71].

And one of the not so articulate nor democratic African leaders, Colonel Acheampong, framed a similar position thus: 'One man, one vote, is meaningless unless accompanied by the principle of 'one man, one bread'[72]. The most forceful response to these and similar positions has come from Africanist left-liberals[73] who have rejected this argument as a smoke-screen for African ruling classes to pursue their authoritarian designs.

Rhoda Howard has disparagingly called it a 'full-belly thesis'. The 'full-belly' thesis is that a man's belly must be full before he can indulge in the 'luxury' of worrying about his political freedoms'[74]. She asserts that political/civil rights are as much a means to an end as ends and goals in themselves as are social and economic rights.

African scholars, on the other hand, have not been as forceful in rejecting the priority of social/economic over political/civil rights. Recognizing that there can be conflicts between these classes of rights in the process of development, they have nonetheless argued for an integrated or comprehensive view of rights. That is to say that no one class of rights has priority over another and that there cannot be a trade-off between political/civil and social/economic rights. 'The requirements of development cannot in any case make us forget respect for human rights, for at the beginning as at the end, the goal of development is the guarantee of human rights'[75].

Comprehensive/integrated *vs* core/basic rights

> One frequently used argument in favour of adopting an integrated approach to human rights, one which treats the right to food at the same time as the right to personal security and the rights to participation, is that there is no point having a full belly if you are not entitled to do anything with the energy derived therefrom, i.e. enjoyment of the right to food in a jail or a zoo is not worth very much. But such an approach falls well short of giving the case for an integrated approach to human rights. The main argument is simply that the continuing enjoyment of, for example the right to food, will almost invariably be dependent upon the enjoyment of other rights such as the right to work and the right to participate in the political process[76].

The fragility of the arguments about the 'comprehensiveness' or the 'integrated' view of all classes of rights is realised and therefore the debate on prioritization continues, albeit in a different form. This time it is between those who assert the integrated view and those who argue in terms of some basic rights. The position on basic rights is argued on different levels. Firstly, it is agreed that one is not creating a hierarchy between classes of rights nor arguing in terms of priority of one set of rights over another. Rather the aim is to identify the basic or irreducible minimum of rights which are the absolute minimum, so to speak, to maintain human dignity and human worth.

Secondly, one level of identifying the minimum is in terms of the minimum of rights while the other level is in terms of the minimum content of rights. One criterion for identifying the minimum is to use, the now fashionable method among Africanists, of relating or basing the minimum of rights on basic needs[77].

For Okoth Ogendo the minimum content, or as he puts it, the irreducible minima, of human rights is:

1. Life in the biological sense.
2. Liberty, to include security of the person or group, freedom of movement and from slavery and servitude.
3. Freedom of conscience, expression, assembly and association.
4. Freedom from discrimination.
5. Self-determination[78].

Rhoda Howard also accepts what she calls a recategorization (as opposed to hierarchy which she opposes) of rights taking her cue from Shue who relates basic rights to basic needs. In her recategorization basic rights are those relating to security and subsistence; those relating to 'human dignity' which include two: 'right to an historically and culturally defined minimum absolute wealth' and right to community; and individual civil and political freedoms and socialist equality[79].

Even the former US Secretary of State, Cyrus Vance, accepts some recategorization of human rights not very dissimilar to Howard's. Vance's three categories are:

> First, there is the right to be free from governmental violation of the person. Such violations include torture; cruel, inhuman, or degrading treatment or punishment; and arbitrary arrest or imprisonment. And they include denial of fair public trial and invasion of the home.
>
> Second, there is the right to the fulfilment of such vital needs as food, shelter, health care, and education. We recognize that the fulfilment of this right will depend, in part, upon the stage of a nation's economic development. But we also know that this right can be violated by a government's action or inaction — for example through corrupt official processes which divert resources to an elite at the expense of the needy or through indifference to the plight of the poor.
>
> Third, there is the right to enjoy civil and political liberties: freedom of thought, of religion, of assembly;

> freedom of speech; freedom of movement both within and outside one's own country; freedom to take part in government[80].

Finally, lately, the debate on the prioritization has been somewhat overshadowed by the discovery of a 'new right' called the 'right to development'. This is discussed in the next section.

'Right to rights': right to development

The 'right to development' is considered a specifically African contribution to the international human rights discourse. Keba M'Baye, a Senegalese jurist, is credited with having first propounded this right in 1972 and later getting it formally recognised in resolution 4(XXXIII) of the UN Commission on Human Rights in 1977 when he presided over its Thirty-third Session[81].

Since then there have been a couple of conferences on the 'right to development' and a score of writings by Africanists on the same, sometimes purporting to expand and elaborate on M'Baye and at other times criticising it. It has also found a formal recognition in the preamble of the African Charter of Human and People's Rights. It was most comprehensively discussed in the UN Secretary General's study entitled: 'The International Dimensions of the Right to Development as a Human Right...'. And finally the UN General Assembly adopted a *Declaration on the Right to Development* by its resolution 41/128 of 4 December 1986[82].

We shall briefly summarise M'Baye's[83] own approach on this right. M'Baye, while not defining development in any precise manner, distinguishes it from growth and argues that development is a metamorphosis of structures involving 'a range of changes in mental and intellectual patterns that favour the rise of growth and its prolongation in historical time'[84]. In short, M'Baye views development as a comprehensive integrated process including, but not confined to, economic development.

He further argues that the right to development is a collective right and belongs to a group. Although he does not seem to stick decisively to this view when he says development concerns 'all men', 'every man' and 'all of man' and therefore it is superfluous 'to indulge in rhetorical speculation on whether the right to development is really a collective or an individual right'[85].

As for the duty-bearers of the right to development, he identifies specifically 'states' and the 'international community'. The right to development 'is a power or prerogative which peoples can demand of their government or of the organized international community'.

The 'father', as M'Baye has been called,[86] of the right of development finds justification for this right on several levels. 'The legitimacy of this right is based on political and economic considerations and is founded on moral grounds and in accordance with legal standards'[87].

Firstly, from the economic standpoint, M'Baye reviews the colonial exploitation of the Third World people by the now developed countries and the continued inequities in the North-South relations. The resultant poverty on the part of the Third World, whose ultimate beneficiaries are the countries of the North, at least gives rise to some obligations on these beneficiaries and therefore, according to M'Baye, a right to development to the people.

Secondly, from the strategic standpoint, M'Baye says, the countries of the North need allies in the underdeveloped world where they put up their military bases. He asserts that many of the wars in this part of the world are proxy wars on behalf of the countries of the developed North.

> It is thus quite clear that in all the conflicts that have occurred since the end of the Second World War, some major power, lurking behind the underdeveloped countries directly involved, has contributed to the conflict, but essentially from a financial standpoint, leaving the losses in human life to the sole responsibility of the underdeveloped countries[88].

From the political standpoint, the countries of the North have been giving tied aid so as to maintain political loyalty and diplomatic constituency in the underdeveloped world in their inter-power rivalries. From this too, it is they who gain.

Then there is also the question of international peace and security. Where the world is divided so dramatically between the rich and the poor, there cannot be a guarantee for peace. Thus the development of the poor is an obligation on the rich.

Fourthly, the rich have the responsibility because international events and their consequences are of their making.

> Since they bring about these events in their interests alone, it is proper, considering that they benefit from the advantages, that they share the disadvantages. They decide on peace and war, the international monetary system, the conditions governing business relations, they impose ideologies, and so on. They tie and untie the knots of

> world politics and the world economy. What could be more natural than that they should assume responsibility for the consequences of events and circumstances that are their own doing? What other justification could there be for the right of veto held by only five States out of the whole family of the United Nations? Some of the events which they have orchestrated as they pleased date back quite far into the past, but their consequences are still dramatically present today. The responsibility for the harm inflicted should be shouldered by those who caused it; it is a matter of elementary justice[89].

But even more important than responsibility, in M'Baye's view, is solidarity. Mankind is gradually moving towards relations based on international solidarity. In this regard too there is a moral justification for the right to development. Those who have must give to those who do not have, only then the principle of solidarity can have any meaning.

Juridically, M'Baye's position seems to be that the right to development is not a new right but is already implied in the various UN instruments and the existing international Covenants on human rights. He cites the *UN Charter* and the UN *Declaration on Human Rights* as having recognised both the limitations on state sovereignty as well as the duty of co-operation. The International Covenants, recognizing various economic, social and cultural rights, and the *Charter of Economic Rights and Duties of States,* all have in one form or another implied the right to development. Thus M'Baye concludes that the right to development has descended from the 'sphere of morals to that of law'[90].

M'Baye's position has variously been re-interpreted by those who purportedly follow him while being dismissed outright by a few others. In the hands of Africanist-liberals the right to development has tended to assume very legalistic formulations, devoid of its political and moral sting, and in some respects rendered conceptually confused by extending it to every one and everywhere[91]. Some of these aspects are reflected in the Draft Working Papers of the UN Commission on Human Rights which was charged with drafting a Declaration on the right to development.

While the Cuban Draft retained some of the political foundations of the M'Baye proposal and defined the right to development as 'an inalienable collective right belonging to all people', the draft of the government experts from the 'Group of 77' defined the 'right to development' as a human right which applies to 'individuals, groups, peoples and States' and 'applicable at the local, national, regional and global level' with even greater emphasis on States[92]. The International Commission of Jurists Draft, which claimed to have only synthesized the Cuban and the 'Group of 77' drafts and put them in a more 'consistent' (and presumably elegant) drafting language, summed up the state-of-the-art. Let us just quote the three basic conceptual and foundation articles:

> Article 1.
>
> 1. The right to development is a right of individuals, groups, peoples and States to participate in and benefit from a process of development aimed at realizing the full potentialities of each person in harmony with the community.
> 2. The right to development recognizes that the human person is the subject as well as the object of development, its main participant as well as its beneficiary.
>
> Article 2.
>
> All human rights, economic, social and cultural, as well as civil and political are interdependent and inseparable elements of the right to development.
>
> Article 3.
>
> The right to development applies at all levels, community, local, national, regional and global.

The breadth and comprehensiveness of the 'right to development' has sometimes attracted to itself the label of 'right to rights' in which case it has been derided by the critics as 'entirely pointless'[93]. In one of the sharpest critiques, Jack Donnelly, using largely M'Baye's article summarised here and the Secretary General's Report, has argued that M'Baye has completely failed to establish the conceptual foundations of the alleged right. His position is that in M'Baye, there is a confusion between the concept of right as an entitlement or claim by specified right-holders against identifiable duty-bearers, and moral righteousness; that all that which may be morally desirable does not necessarily and even eventually constitute a right, moral or legal.

Further, that in the existing Covenants, UN Declarations and intergovernmental treaties — except for the African Charter — there is no such right, and certainly not a collective right, to development. Donnelly concludes that the whole hullabaloo about the right to development is just another stratagem by developing states to press for greater aid and assistance from the developed North; to justify their demands for a New International Economic Order; to deflect attention from their violations of political/civil rights and to smuggle in the priority of economic/social-rights argument through the back door[94].

Many of the African scholars, on the other hand, have accepted the existence and validity of the right to development without much challenge or discussion[95]. Those of a more critical bent, while accepting the desirability of such a right, have nevertheless argued that such a right cannot be said to exist in international law[96]. Vojin Dimitrijevic has summed up this position in a theoretically sophisticated fashion:

> The formation of values precedes the formulation of legal norms, but values may be expressed in normative form. Such an expression can symbolise the desire for a new situation, with all its undertones — this is where I think the right to development should be presently located. It suffices then to show that there is a broadly held belief that individuals and peoples have a right to development. This belief will certainly act as a principle which will shape many decisions and concrete legal provisions in the future[97].

The UN General Assembly has finally adopted a resolution 41/128 of 4 December 1986 called the 'Declaration on the Right to Development'. In consonance with UN and general position of the Afro-Asian states, the Declaration is strictly state-centric. We will have occasion to look at it more closely in Chapter Three below.

PROMOTION, PREVENTION AND EXPOSITION

Over the last two decades, human rights talk has proliferated the Western scene, both diplomatic and academic[98]. The gruesome massacres in Uganda[99], Equatorial Guinea[100] and Bokassa's Central African Empire have attracted a lot of international publicity relating to the question of human rights in Africa. There is then of course the omnipresent and the most naked violation of human rights in South Africa which is intrinsically linked to national liberation in that part of the world.

In this human rights activity, the most active organisations have been non-governmental organisations (NGOs) and individual human rights activists at various levels, both organised as well as individuals in academia. In this section, we briefly survey the scene in Africa at various levels of human rights activity.

For the purposes of our exposition, we divide the agencies involved in human rights activity into the following. First, there are the inter-governmental organisations (IGOs). These are those set up by some agreement between and among states. Among these may also be included UN organisations and agencies connected with human rights questions. In Africa much ink has been spilt over adopting a Regional Human Rights Charter and setting up a regional human rights body.

In this process the UN Commission on Human Rights, African jurists, particularly the African Bar Association, and Western liberals and activist organisations have been quite active. The African Charter on Human and People's Rights was finally adopted in 1981 and just a year ago an eleven-men African Commission was elected by the Assembly of Heads of State. I will return to the Charter in greater detail later.

Besides the IGOs there are the NGOs. The NGOs may be divided into three major groups. The International (or sometimes called transnational) Non-governmental Organisations (INGOs), the foreign based NGOs but active on African questions (FONGOs) and the local NGOs (LONGOs). Among the INGOs may be mentioned such groups as the International Commission of Jurists (ICJ) based in Geneva; the Swiss based International Committee of the Red Cross (ICRC); the American based International League for Human Rights and the well-known Amnesty International (AI).

The ICJ consists of 40 prominent lawyers from all over the world, is run by an Executive Committee and has over 50 national sections[101]. It was founded in 1952 in West Berlin, during the hey-day of the cold war, as a counterpart of the Soviet-associated International Association of Democratic Lawyers. Its objective is 'the support and advancement of those principles of justice which constitute the basis of the Rule of Law' and in spite of its political origins, it is said to have kept up with its 'non-political denomination prescribed by its statute'[102]. Among other things, it has been active in Africa in organising conferences, one of its most-quoted ones being on human rights in a one party state held in Dar-es-Salaam in 1976[103].

The ICRC is considered a custodian of the Geneva Convention on armed conflicts and its role in Africa has been mainly in the area of war and in securing humane treatment for prisoners.

The International League for Human Rights is New York-based and was founded in 1942. In 1976, together with the New York Law Associates, it set up the Lawyers Committee for International Human Rights. The latter has produced book-length reports on human rights situations in Uganda, Liberia and Zimbabwe.[104]. It draws its leadership mainly from Americans. Thus the Lawyers Committee is strictly a local American organisation and therefore, in that sense, may be placed under FONGOs.

Founded in 1961 to do something about the 'forgotten prisoners', the AI has grown world-wide although it remains primarily a European-based group[105]. Amnesty International has reported actively on human rights violations in Africa besides mounting specific campaigns on such issues as tortures etc. As of 1986, AI had four sections in Africa — in Ghana, Ivory Coast, Nigeria and Senegal and some five groups — Egypt, Mauritius, Sierra Leone, Tanzania and Zambia[106]. But these sections and groups, by virtue of the AI Statutes, cannot involve themselves in any local human rights issues.

Finally, mention may be made of two organisations of probably greatest interest and relevance to Africa but least publicised in the West. These are the Bertrand Russell Tribunals which organised the Vietnam War Crimes Tribunals and the Rome-based Lelio Basso Foundation for the Rights and Liberation of Peoples which sponsored the 1976 Algiers Declaration on the Rights of Peoples to which we shall return at the appropriate place.

The FONGOs are those based outside Africa but with international human rights concerns. Such, for example, is the Human Rights Internet whose main function is to produce an up-to-date reportage on human rights developments including developments in the NGO world all over the world. There are numerous other issue-oriented or country-based organisations in Europe and North America which need not detain us[107].

LONGOs are locally organised NGOs concerned with human rights and related questions, based either in an individual African country or on a Pan-African basis. Although we did not come across a systematic study of this on an African level, it is fair to say that there are very few LONGOs in Africa compared to even say Latin America or Asia.

As a matter of fact, as I said earlier, much of the efforts of African human rights activists has gone into creating an inter-state organ rather than local NGOs. Nevertheless a few do exist. First there are church-based or related organisations. The African Church has not always been in the forefront of human rights struggles. The involvement of the Church and the Muslim community in South Africa in this regard is unique and exceptional[108]. The All Africa Council of Churches[109]; Churches in Kenya, Uganda and Zimbabwe (the Catholic Commission for Justice and Peace) have on and off taken up human rights questions.

The other set of LONGOs have been related to law and legal activities. Among these are the various legal aid groups. The Legal Aid Committee of the Faculty of Law, University of Dar-es-Salaam, the Legal Advice Center and the Public Law Institute of Kenya, the

Zimbabwe Association of Democratic Jurists are among the few that may be mentioned. Their activities, unlike for instance various such groups in South Africa, have been sporadic and somewhat inconsistent.

There are also a few African Bar associations, for example the Ghanaian[110], which have on and off taken up some human rights questions in their countries. However these have been largely issues to do with legal procedures, independence of the judiciary, existence of the private bar and so on[111].

Specifically human rights committees or other forms of organised human rights groups are rare in Africa[112]. Where they do exist, they inevitably attract repression from the regimes. The Algerian League of Human Rights, the Tunisian National Council for Public Liberty[113] and the Senegal Institute of Human Rights are among the few that still exist.

If there is such a dearth of active human rights NGOs in African countries, the picture on the pan-African level is even worse. The African Bar Association has been active but its activities have been largely confined to questions related to rule of law and seems to have done very little in regard to exposition of human rights violations in Africa. Recently, after many years of seminars and conferences, an African body was launched in Harare called the African Association of Human and Peoples Rights in Development (AAHRID). It is too early to say what will be the impact of this new organisation. Its constitution embraces everything that is current in the human rights discourse on Africa and sets itself, among other things, the task of exposing human rights violations in Africa.

Meanwhile, another pan-African organisation called the Panafrican Center for Research on Peace, Development and Human Rights (PARCEP) has been set up in Nigeria[114]. Its accent is on research and related intellectual pursuits in the area of linkages between peace, development and human rights. It sees for itself an activist role in that it seeks to 'promote policy recommendations arising from research findings' and 'sell such recommendations to the relevant African governments and population'.

As for the activities of the INGOs and FONGOs, it has been largely in the area of promotion and exposition of violations of human rights. Promotion has been mainly, if not exclusively, in terms of organising seminars, conferences and workshops to which African academics, usually jurists, are invited. There has been much expository literature on violations emanating from INGOs and FONGOs. African LONGOs, on the other hand, have been slow and dilatory on both fronts and least active in practical human rights work at the grass-root level. Much of the human rights related writing of Africans is to be found in scholarly journals, usually foreign, and addressed to foreign audiences.

NOTES

1. Josiah A.M. Cobbah, 'African Values and the Human Rights Debate: An African Perspective', *Human Rights Quarterly* 9, no.3:309-331 (Aug.1987).
2. This probably does not include Latin American writers with respect to this particular debate. Culturally the dominant Latin American view would seem to identify itself with European values. See, for instance, Heleno Fragoso's (a former vice-president of the Brazilian Bar Association) positions at the Bellagio Conference where he argued that while the economic problems and conditions of Latin America resembled those of Asia and Africa, Latin America had a foot in two worlds. Like North America, Latin America could claim to be the legatee of European traditions and ideals. The Conference proceedings are in Malcolm Richardson (ed.), *Human Rights, Human Needs, and Developing Nations* (The Rockefeller Foundation, May 1980), p.36.
3. See generally Yougindra Khushalani, 'Human Rights in Asia and Africa', *Human Rights Law Journal* 4, no.4:403-442 (1983).
4. Rhoda E. Howard, *Human Rights in Commonwealth Africa* (New Jersey: Rowman & Littlefield, 1986), p.23.
5. *Ibid.*, p.17.
6. Cited *ibid.*
7. Edward Kannyo, *Human Rights in Africa: Problems and Prospects*, A Report Prepared for the International League for Human Rights, May 1980, p.4.
8. Quoted in Hurst Hannum,'The Butare Colloquium on Human Rights and Economic Development in Francophone Africa: A Summary and Analysis', *Universal Human Rights* 1, no.2:63-87 at p.82, fn. 67.
9. Khushalani, op.cit., p.414; Dunstan Wai in Richardson, *op.cit.*, pp.43 *et.seq.*; Lakshman Marasinghe, 'Traditional Conceptions of Human Rights in Africa', in Claude E. Welch, Jr. & Ronald I. Meltzer (eds.), *Human Rights and Development in Africa* (Albany: State University of New York Press, 1984), p.32; Adamantia Pollis, 'Liberal, Socialist, and Third World Perspectives of Human Rights', in Peter Schwab & Adamantia Pollis (eds.), *Toward a Human Rights Framework* (New York: Praegar, 1982), p.1 *et.seq.*
10. Adamantia Pollis, *ibid.*, p.16.
11. Howard, *op.cit.*, p.25.
12. Keba M'Baye and Birame Ndiaye, 'The Organization of African Unity (OAU)', in Philip Alston, *The International Dimensions of Human Rights* (Westport, Connecticut: Greenwood Press & Paris, — UNESCO, 1982), p.583.
13. In Richardson (ed.), *op.cit.*
14. M'Baye, *op.cit.*, p.588.
15. Osita C. Eze, *Human Rights in Africa: Some Selected Problems* (Lagos: Nigerian Institute of International Affairs & Macmillan Nigeria Publishers Ltd.,1984), ch.2. This book has a different approach from the 'mainstream'; no wonder it has been largely ignored.
16. *Op.cit.*
17. *Ibid.*, p.331.
18. Fasil Nahum, 'African Contribution to Human Rights'. Paper presented to the *African Seminar on Human Rights and Development*, National Institute of Development Research and Documentation, University of Botswana, Gaborone, May 24-29, 1982, hereinafter referred to as the 'Gaborone Seminar'. I am grateful to Paul Martin of the Columbia Human Rights Center for making the mimeographed version of these papers available to me.

19. Abdullahi A. Al-Na'im, 'Religious Minorities under Islamic Law and the Limits of Cultural Relativism', *Human Rights Quarterly* 9, no.1:1-18 at p.18 (Feb.1987). See also his article 'A Modern Approach to Human Rights in Islam: Foundations and Implications for Africa' in Welch & Meltzer (eds.), *op.cit.*, p.75.
20. Howard, *op.cit.*, p.17.
21. See, for instance, Claude E. Welch, Jr., 'Human Rights as a Problem in Contemporary Africa', in Welch & Meltzer (eds.), *op.cit.*, p.11.
22. Hurst Hannum, *op.cit.*, p.67.
23. In an excellent work, referred to again below, Hountondji argues that African philosophy is that literature produced by Africans (geographically speaking) about philosophical problems. *Ethnophilosophy* on the other hand is the literature, pretending to be philosophical, about what the Africanists consider to be the world-view of traditional Africa, Paulin J. Hountondji, *African Philosophy: Myth and Reality* (London: Hutchinson University Library for Africa, 1983), ch.3.
24. K. R. Minogue, 'Natural Rights, Ideology and the Game of Life', in Eugene Kamenka & Alice Erh-Soon Tay (eds.), *Human Rights* (London: Edward Arnold, 1978), p.13 at p.17; Tom Campbell, 'Introduction: Realizing Human Rights', in Tom Campbell *et.al* (eds.), *Human Rights from Rhetoric to Reality* (Oxford & New York: Blackwell, 1986), p.1 and Alan S. Rosenbaum, 'Introduction', in Alan S. Rosenbaum (ed.), *The Philosophy of Human Rights: International Perspectives* (Westport, Connecticut: Greenwood Press, 1980), p.8.
25. This is the famous phrase from Jeremy Bentham quoted in Richardson (ed.), *op.cit.*, p.6.
26. Rosenbaum, *op.cit.*, p.19.
27. In Kelsen's 'pure theory of law' grundnorm is the ultimate from which other norms are derived and the social category 'state' has no place in his logical system. But once logic is related to life, it is clear that the ultimate source of Kelsenian norms cannot be anything but the state. It is the spurious separation of life from logic that obliges Kelsen to resort to a fiction in a self-declared scientific theory. For Kelsen's theories see Lloyd, *Introduction to Jurisprudence* (London: Stevens, 1979), 4th edn., pp.307-28.
28. For Fuller-Hart debate see LLoyd, *op.cit.*, pp.252-9.
29. Ronald Dworkin, *Taking Rights Seriously* (Cambridge: Harvard University Press, 1977).
30. John Rawls, *A Theory of Justice* (Cambridge: Harvard University press, 1973). For an excellent exposition of Rawls metaphysics see D.P. Chattopadhyaya, 'Human Rights, Justice, and Social Context', in Alan S. Rosenbaum, *op.cit.*, pp.169-91. Chattopadhyaya's critique of Rawls is *mutatis mutandis* applicable to Dworkin.
31. Hermann Klenner, 'Human Rights: A Battle-cry for Social Change or a Challenge to Philosophy of Law?', paper circulated at the World Congress on Philosophy of Law and Social Philosophy, Sydney/Canberra, Aug. 1977, pp. 8-9, quoted in Alice Erh-Soon Tay, 'Marxism, socialism and human rights', in Kamenka & Tay (eds.), *op.cit.* p.104.
32. Imre Szabo, 'The theoretical foundations of human rights', in Asbjorn Eide & August Schou (eds.), *International Protection of Human Rights: Proceedings of the Seventh Nobel Symposium*, Oslo Sep. 25-27, 1967 (New York: Interscience Publishers, 1968), p.37.

    In international life human rights are first manifest as claims, postulates, in the wake of the citizens' rights passing into positive international law. Thus we first encounter them as international legal claims, next turning into incomplete positive international law in the Universal Declaration of Human Rights, and subsequently into complete ones in the international treaties relating to human rights. In international relations the term 'rights' is applied both to the pretensions demanding to be recognized in positive international law, and to the positive international law in which such 'rights' are already substantiated. *Ibid.*

33. See, for instance, John Kleinig, 'Human Rights, Legal Rights and Social Change', in Kamenka & Tay, (eds.), *op.cit.*, pp.37-46.
34. See, *inter alia*, Robert Martin, *Personal Freedom and the Law in Tanzania* (Nairobi: Oxford University Press, 1974); *Eastern Africa Law Review* 11-14, Special Issue on 'The State and the Constitution' (Dar-es-Salaam: University of Dar-es-Salaam, Faculty of Law) and Ekwueme Okoli, 'Toward a Human Rights Framework in Nigeria', in Schwab & Pollis (eds.), *op.cit.*, pp.203-21; Larry Diamond, 'Issues in the Constitutional Design of a Third Nigerian Republic', *African Affairs*, April 1987.
35. But see B.O. Nwabueze, *Constitutionalism in Emergent States* (New Jersey: Fairleigh Dickinson University Press, 1973); Howard, op.cit, p.164 *et seq.* and Martin Dent, 'Three Constitutions Compared', *West Africa* 25 November, 1979.
36. For a bibliography see Welch & Meltzer (eds.) *op.cit.*, pp.301-06.
37. See generally Franck Moderne, 'The influence of the U.S. conception of human rights in the post-independence colonial constitutions: the example of the English-speaking and French-speaking Black Africa', (University of Paris I, mimeo. n.d.).
38. Legal Aid Committee, *Essays in Law and Society*, (Dar-es-Salaam: Faculty of Law, 1985), pp.12-3.
39. See Howard, *op.cit.*, p.164 *et seq.*
40. Issa G. Shivji, 'The State of the Constitution and the Constitution of the State in Tanzania', *Eastern Africa Law Review* 11-14, op.cit., pp.1-34.
41. *Cf.* 'The Law of Lagos' adopted by 194 judges, practising lawyers and teachers of law from 23 African countries and 9 of other continents under the auspices of the International Commission of Jurists, reproduced in Ian Brownlie, *Basic Documents on Human Rights* (Oxford University Press, 1981) 2nd edn., pp.426-37.
42. Welch & Meltzer (eds.) *op.cit.*, Appendix Three, pp.338-9, list some 18 African conferences between 1961 and 1981 on Human Rights.
43. See Chattopadhyaya, *op.cit.*
44. Margaret Macdonald, 'Natural Rights' in Jeremy Waldron (ed.) *Theories of Rights* (London: Oxford University Press. 1984), p.27.
45. Maurice Cranston, *What are Human Rights*? (London: The Bodley Head, 1973), ch.1. This book is representative of a liberal position on human rights, if somewhat simplified.
46. This is Maurice Cranston's definition quoted in Richardson (ed.), *op.cit.*, p.7.
47. Eze, *op.cit.*, p.4.
48. Andrew Levin, 'Human Rights', in Alan S. Rosenbaum (ed.), *op.cit*, p.137.
49. *Op.cit.*, p.218.
50. *Ibid.*, p.16.
51. Kannyo, *Human Rights*, *op.cit.*, p.4.
52. Szabo, 'Foundations', *op.cit.*, p.36.
53. *Op.cit.*, p.320.
54. See M'Baye, 'OAU', *op.cit.*, p.589. M'Baye does not seem to understand the 'traditional' concept of 'obligation' and has imported Hohfeldian conception through the back door.
55. Eze, *op.cit.*, pp. 5-6.
56. Welch, *'Human Rights as a Problem'*, *op.cit.*, p.26.

57. H.S.Kibola, 'Some Conceptual Aspects of Human Rights: The Basis for the Right to Development in Africa', paper presented to the Gaborone Seminar, *op.cit.*, p.5.
58. See generally Imre Szabo (ed.), *Socialist Concept of Human Rights* (Institute for Legal and Administrative Sciences of the Hungarian Academy of Sciences, n.d.).
59. For further discussion on this see chapters three and four below.
60. *Cf.* Welch, 'Human Rights as a Problem', *op.cit.*, p.16. On the African state position on self-determination see below ch.4.
61. For texts of these Covenants see Brownlie, *op.cit.*, pp.118 and 128 respectively.
62. See Ian Brownlie, *Principles of Public International Law* (Oxford: Clarendon Press, 1979) 3rd.edn., pp.593-6; G.I.Tunkin (ed.), *International Law, A Textbook* (Moscow: Progress Publishers, 1986), pp.141-4 and Eze, *op.cit.*
63. See the discussion on this in Eide & Schou (eds.), *op.cit.*, p.283. The quotation represents Capotorti's and probably also Fawcett's position. For the position of U.K., France and the U.S.A. on this and their argument that collective, territorial rights had no place in the Covenant see Rhoda Howard, 'The Dilemma of Human Rights in Sub-Saharan Africa', *International Journal* 3, no.4:724-47 at p.735 (Autumn, 1980).
64. See Howard, *op.cit.*, p.16. See also her article 'The Dilemma', op.cit.
65. Philip Elston & Asbjorn Eide, 'Discussion Paper prepared for the African Seminar on Human Rights and Development', Gaborone Seminar, *op.cit.*, p.2.
66. *Ibid.*, p.8.
67. See H.W.O. Okoth-Ogendo, 'National Implementation of International Responsibility: Some Thoughts on Human Rights in Africa', paper presented to the Gaborone Seminar, *op.cit.*
68. Brownlie, *Human Rights, op. cit.*, p.242. See Obinna B. Okere, 'The Protection of Human Rights in Africa and the African Charter on Human and People's Rights: A Comparative Analysis with the European and American Systems', *Human Rights Quarterly* 6, no.2:141-59 (May, 1984).
69. Szabo, 'Foundations', *op.cit.*, p.42.
70. Quoted in M'Baye, 'OAU', *op.cit.*, p.588.
71. Julius K. Nyerere, 'Stability and Change in Africa', printed in *Africa Contemporary Record* 2 (1969-70), C30-31.
72. Quoted in Rhoda Howard, 'The Full-Belly Thesis: Should Economic Rights Take Priority Over Civil and Political Rights? Evidence from Sub-Saharan Africa', *Human Rights Quarterly* 5, no.4:467-90 at p.467 (November, 1983).
73. See, *inter alia,* the editors' 'ASEAN Perspectives on Human Rights', in Harry M. Scoble & Laurie S. Wiseberg (eds.), *Access to Justice: Human Rights Struggles in South East Asia* (London: Zed Books Ltd., 1985), pp.3-8.
74. 'Full-Belly Thesis', *op.cit.*, p.469.
75. Seminega, 'Human Rights and Development', p.29 quoted in Hannum, *op.cit.*, p.70.
76. Alston & Eide, *op.cit.*, p.47.
77. Why should Western Africanists think their 'basic needs' thesis such a great discovery beats imagination, unless it is just another of those fads!
78. Okoth Ogendo, *op.cit.*, p.2.
79. 'Full-Belly Thesis', *op.cit.*, pp.488-89.
80. Quoted in Richard Falk, 'Comparative Protection of Human Rights in Capitalist and Socialist Third World Countries', *Universal Human Rights* 1, no.2:3-29 at p.17 (April-June, 1979).
81. Jack Donnelly, 'The 'Right to Development': How Not to Link Rights and Development', in Welch & Meltzer (eds.), *op.cit.*, p.261.

82. The text is reprinted in the International Commission of Jurists, *The Review*, no.38:53-6 (June 1987).
83. Keba M'Baye, 'Emergence of the 'Right to Development' as a Human Right in the Context of a New International Economic Order', paper presented to the UNESCO Meeting of Experts on Human Rights, Human Needs and the Establishment of a New International Economic Order, Paris, UNESCO, 19-23 June 1978, Doc. SS-78/CONF.630/8.
84. This is a quotation from J.Austruy approvingly quoted by M'Baye, *ibid.*, p.4.
85. *Ibid.*, p.2.
86. Alston and Eide, *op.cit.*, p.51.
87. *Ibid.*, p.5.
88. *Ibid.*, p.7.
89. *Ibid.*, p.9.
90. *Ibid.*, p.14.
91. See Alston and Eide, *op.cit.*, generally.
92. The Working Papers including the Cuban and the ICJ drafts are to be found in the papers of the Gaborone Seminar, *op.cit.*
93. Donnelly, *op.cit.*, p.273.
94. *Ibid.*
95. See the conclusions of the Butare Colloquium in Hannum, *op.cit.*, p.69.
96. See, for instance, U. O. Umozurike, 'The African Charter of Human and People's Rights and the Rights to development', paper presented to the Gaborone Seminar, *op.cit.*
97. Vojin Dimitrijevic, 'Development as a Right', paper presented at the Gaborone Seminar, *op.cit.*, p.4.
98. Laurie S. Wiseberg & Harry M. Scoble, 'Recent Trends in the Expanding Universe of NGOs Dedicated to the Protection of Human Rights', in Ved P. Nanda *et al.*, *Global Human Rights: Public Policies, Comparative Measures and NGO Strategies* (Boulder, Colorado: Westview Press, 1981), p.229.
99. See Amnesty International publications: AI, USA, 'Human Rights in Uganda', (June 1978); *Uganda: Evidence of Torture*, June 1985 and AI, England, 'Human Rights in Uganda; Extra Judicial Executions, Torture and Political Imprisonment', September, 1982.
100. Randall Fegley, 'The U.N. Human Rights Commission: The Equatorial Guinea Case', *Human Rights Quarterly* 3, no.1:34-47 (Feb. 1981).
101. Nigel S. Rodley, 'Monitoring Human Rights', in Jorge I. Dominguez *et.al.*, *Enhancing Human Rights* (New York: McGraw Hill Book, 1979), pp.117-51 at p.141.
102. *Ibid.*
103. For proceedings and papers see ICJ, *Human Rights in a One Party State* (London: Search Press, 1978).
104. Lawyers Committee for Human Rights, 'Violations of Human Rights in Uganda 1971-78', June 15, 1978; *Zimbabwe: Wages of War* (New York: 1986) and *Liberia: A Promise Betrayed* (New York: 1986).
105. Nigel S. Rodley, 'Monitoring Human Rights', in Jorge I. Dominguez *et al.*, *Enhancing Human Rights* (New York: McGraw Hill Books, 1979), pp.117-151 at p.140.
106. See AI's 1987 Report, pp.387-9.
107. See generally Harry S. Scoble, 'Human Rights Non-Governmental Organizations in Black Africa: Their Problems and Prospects in the Wake of Banjul Charter', in Welch & Meltzer, *op.cit.*, pp.177-225.
108. *Africa Events*, (citation misplaced)

109. The statement entitled 'Factors Responsible for the Violation of Human Rights in Africa', issued by the All Africa Council of Churches meeting in Khartoum, Feb.16-22, 1975 is even radical. Reprinted in *Issue: A Quarterly Journal of Africanist Opinion* 6, no.4:44-6 (Winter 1976).
110. See an untitled article by Edward Kannyo published by The Jacob Blaustein Institute for the Advancement of Human Rights, 1980.
111. For the boycott of the Public Tribunals by the Ghana bar see AI, USA: *The Public Tribunals in Ghana*, 1984.
112. Scoble, *op.cit.* The author, however, gives some obscurantist reasons for their absence.
113. Wiseberg & Scoble, *op.cit.*, p.238.
114. *The Codesria Bulletin*, vol.viii, no.3, 1987.

2. A CRITIQUE

HUMAN RIGHTS IDEOLOGY: PHILOSOPHICAL IDEALISM AND POLITICAL NIHILISM

The prevailing human rights discourse on Africa, as I have endeavoured to highlight in Chapter One, is fundamentally within the idealist philosophical world outlook. It is abstracted from social history and thereby arrives at conclusions which make human rights both eternal in historical time and universal in social space. This is not to say that it does not admit history at all. It does. Its conception of history though is a 'history' of ideas, events and persons, not social history which, among other things, is based on material conditions of life, social processes and economic relationships. The idealist approaches of the discussants are best illustrated by the debate on the universalism of human rights concepts as well as on the theoretical conceptualisation of 'human nature' and 'rights'.

Human rights concepts are traced back to the classical Greek period. 'Philosophers as a rule trace the human rights idea (sic) back to its philosophical inception in classical Athenian democracy and in the Stoical influence on Roman jurisprudence'[1]. The development of the idea is then followed through the natural law theories of the Middle Ages, the natural rights of the seventeenth century and the secular period of Enlightenment right up to the revival of natural law in the post-world war II period. The moral or the message of this 'history' is to demonstrate that the idea or the concept of human rights has existed from eternity (which incidentally seems to begin with the beginning of European history). As one critic puts it:

> It is held by these scholars, summarized briefly, that the 1789 French Declaration of the 'rights of man and citizen' closed a two-thousand years old, uninterrupted evolution, for the idea of human rights had been part of the political thinking ever since the time of Stoa, consequential upon Rome having adopted the concept of equality which is of Stoic origin[2].

However, it is admitted that the idea of human rights has undergone changes in its content and formulation in its long voyage. These changes are then discussed at great length and almost invariably conclude that the modern conception of human rights is a kind of perfected version, valid for and applicable to the whole of humanity and therefore universal. Of course, in the good tradition of liberalism and pluralism, differences and debate on the modern universal conception are not only admitted but vigorously pursued as a further illustration of its liberal, democratic and universal character.

At one extreme of this debate is the left-liberal view which departs from the liberal letter, if not the spirit, by recognising that the human rights idea is related to and reflects socio-economic conditions. Historically it is Western liberal in origin. Conceptually, it is a reflection, on the moral and legal planes, of the individualised, commodity society associated with the development of capitalism in the West. Since Western colonialism has more or less universalized commodity production and capitalist relations in the former African colonies, it is further argued, then only the Western liberal view of human rights, which is intended to and can safeguard the individual against the state, is applicable and valid in Africa. Therefore it is universal.[3]

In its leftism, this view goes even further and argues, in part correctly, that the cultural-relativist conception of human rights is an ideological justification of the authoritarianism of the African ruling classes. But this is a partial and one-sided view, for while it recognises the class and ideological character of the cultural-relativist position (the left element in its left-liberalism), it fails to discern the ideological character in its own universalist position. It sees classes but abstracts them from class struggle, particularly in relation to the imperialist domination of Africa. For a leading left-liberal, Rhoda, '... revolution seems not to be a realistic political option in present-day Commonwealth Africa'[4]. As we shall argue in detail later, according to this position demands for human rights are seen as absolutes and therefore constant rather than as a part of the process of struggle for transformation. Thus its outlook suffers from a metaphysical orientation and is therefore still located and locked within the paradigms of philosophical idealism.

The cultural-relativist position, which concentrates on showing that traditional African societies have also had conceptions of human rights, similarly suffers from philosophical idealism. It fails to understand the correct material and philosophical basis of certain community-oriented conceptions and practices in some of the more or less classless societies in Africa; portrays these as human rights and endeavours to prove that they are similar to Western human rights.

Politically, this viewpoint does not even have a nationalist (used in the sense to be discussed below) character and betrays a colonial-type cultural inferiority. Put rhetorically, to show that we too are humans we do not have to abandon being Africans nor show that our humanity is similar to the humanity of Western capitalist society. Indeed, why do we have to show that we are humans? In spite of the assertions of cultural-relativists, I suggest here and will show later, that their standpoint is objectively compradorial and its conceptual distance from the Western liberal view is insignificant.

Conceptually, the dominant outlook on 'human rights' centres around the concept of 'human nature'. Human nature is an abstraction both from history as well as society. The historically determined social being, abstracted from social-history, is transformed into a human being in general while material social relations, abstracted from political economy, are metamorphosed into a bundle of ideal qualities and characteristics called 'human nature'. The 'human nature' so arrived at philosophically is ideologically declared more-or-less eternal, more-or-less immutable, at least in its fundamentals. The discourse is strictly compartmentalised as philosophical and therefore politically and ideologically neutral while morally and ethically it is preached as righteous. The process of positivising these moral rights into statutory/treaty law is part of human rights activity in which the human rights community is engaged. The human rights community is constituted by an amalgam of supposedly non-political philosophers, jurists, political scientists, academics etc. in collectives called non-governmental organisations.

Within Western idealist philosophy, human rights concepts have been broadly located in two major traditions — natural law and positivism[5]. The development of natural law itself may be periodized into four periods — the classical, the medieval, renaissance and enlightenment and the post-World War II revivalism. Arguing that justice is the most abstract form of natural right, Engels notes that 'justice is but the ideologised, glorified expression of the existing economic relations, now from their conservative, and now from their revolutionary angle'[6].

The same can be said of natural law. In its conservative role, natural law justifies the existing order by providing a divine sanctity to the rulers and their laws[7] while, in its revolutionary role, it provides a mobilizing ideology to the rising classes for the overthrow of the existing order. In both cases, natural law theories, and their later-day derivative, 'natural rights' theories, are essentially political, class-based ideologies, here playing a legitimising and there playing a mobilising role.

In the classical and medieval periods, natural law played largely a conservative role to justify the existing order of political and economic inequalities. The philosopher-king of Plato is naturally endowed as a ruler while the equality of the Athenian city-state naturally does not extend to its slave population. Under the Greeks, natural law is still parochial. It is only under Roman imperialism that the needs of commerce, conquest and rule over foreigners lend it a universalistic character in the form of *jus gentium.* The Roman rulers applied their *jus civile,* stripped of formalities, to their Empire and the Roman jurists/ideologists obliged by giving it the legitimacy of the law of nature which the Stoics had earlier declared to be universally applicable[8].

During the middle ages, perched on the edifice of feudalism, natural law sanctified hierarchy as well as justified the supremacy of the Catholic Church. And Thomas Aquinas worked out a neat compromise which, while maintaining the supremacy of the Church, removed the stigma of the original sin from the civil government. But this was a tenuous compromise for tension between the Church and the state remained. It is important to stress that the natural laws of the classical and medieval periods had little in common between them except the name and they in turn are far removed, both in content and social character, from the natural rights theories of the bourgeois revolutions.

During the long-drawn out bourgeois revolutions, natural law, and its derivative natural rights, played a revolutionary role against the *status quo* and in the interests of the rising middle classes. The compromises reached between the English aristocracy and the English bourgeoisie facilitated the entry of the English bourgeois revolution onto the historical stage through the Parliament bringing with it the whole traditional baggage, including the Englishman's feudal parochialism. Thus the English Petition of Rights, 1627 and the English Bill of Rights of 1679 were exclusively for the Englishman. Locke used natural law as the foundation of his theory of natural rights to life, liberty and property providing ideological justification for the Glorious Revolution (1688) and for the rights of the Englishmen[9]. A century later, the much more decisive French revolution, taking place against the background of absolutism, universalized the language of rights by declaring the Rights of Man and Citizen in 1789.

The American Declaration too adopted a universal language. But the declared universality was fundamentally ideological. Language did not correspond to life. 'Man' did not include 'woman' nor 'slave'. If the eighteenth century declarations of rights of man did not include all men, the twentieth century conceptions have not been that universalistic either[10]. In the era of colonialism, the definition of 'man' has not included the 'colonial man' and the 'native' has been excluded from the notion of 'citizen'[11].

The rise of the concept of an autonomous individual with the advent of capitalism has often been noted. In the liberal conceptions of human rights, rights attach to the erstwhile individual. The commodity owner of the market thus becomes the juristic subject of law and bearer of rights, simultaneously constituting the human being of moral philosophy and the glorious individual of liberalism. The concept and language of rights in law and morality, whose fundamental basis is the standard of equality, is an expression of the equivalence of exchange in the sphere of commodity circulation. The free and equal commodity-owner of the market, who enters into equally free and equal exchange relations, translates itself into the free and equal juristic person as the holder of a bundle of rights, who freely enters into legal relations through a contract[12].

Thus the language of rights in human rights is related to a commodity producing society which necessarily dissolves the bondage of natural-economy societies based on tradition and community. Simultaneously, as Marx explained, the realm of political organisation, the state, separates from civil society. With the further development of bourgeois society, the state perfects itself as the military-bureaucratic machine whose most developed form is the highly militarised modern imperialist state[13]. As in life the imperialist state develops more and more, becoming hegemonic over civil society, so in language the chasm between civil/political rights and their substratum in the life-processes of the world of production becomes wider and deeper. Here too the pretences about the universality of the civil/political rights translate into imperialist practices of their suppression, as we shall see later. Before examining these issues in some detail, let us turn to the other Western tradition, positivism.

If the ideology of natural-rights was the rallying cry of the rising bourgeoisie against feudalism, positivism became the ideology of the triumphant bourgeoisie. Through it the bourgeoisie declared not only its victory but its resolution to stay and build the world in its own image. There were no more ideals to fight for, the 'is' was the 'ought' and therefore there was no need to look beyond the existing law and state. Rights were those granted by the state and all talk about inherent rights was nothing but metaphysical.

In Kelsen's writings logical legal positivism reached its apogee. He argued that law was essentially a system of norms governed by rules of logic. In this system it was not 'rights' but 'obligations' which occupied the centre-stage as 'rights' were simply a reflection, and even then a pale one, of 'duties'. Kelsen, in his onslaught on the theories of natural law and the sociological school, argued that natural or inherent rights had simply been ideological constructs in defence of private property. One can hardly take exception to the latter part of the statement; but otherwise Kelsen took positivism to its absurd conclusions by asserting that law could be understood and explained within law. In his 'science' of law, which he called the Pure Theory of Law, Kelsen did away with such 'impurities' as state and society by a process of logical abstraction.

His tools of scientific analysis, to borrow a term from the 'impure' social sciences, were a given number of *a priori* mental categories or concepts which he gracefully borrowed from Kant's metaphysics. He attempted to build his 'science' from such mental constructs and it is no wonder that he ended up creating, by his own admission, a fictitious grundnorm to complete his jigsaw puzzle of logical and hierarchical norms. Laski described this as an 'exercise in logic, not in life'[14] while Pashukanis made a biting critique comparing Kelsen's 'science' with a game of chess[15].

Be that as it may. What is important for our purposes is to underline that positivism, like natural law, was and continues to be, though in a modified form, an ideology of the bourgeoisie both in its content as well as in its methodology. If the natural rights ideology of the Enlightenment was an instrument of change to establish bourgeois rule, positivism is eminently an ideology of the *status quo* to protect bourgeois rule. Natural law in its conservative form justified the political and economic inequalities of the classical and medieval periods, while positivism, which has never had any revolutionary angle, provides justification for the social and economic inequalities of the capitalist era as at the same time majestically proclaiming to be the theoretical fountain-head of political and legal equality. Legal positivism has found expression in the colonial, and now the neo-colonial, jurisprudence in its narrowest form[16].

To be sure, positivism received its rudest shock in Nazism and fascism which found the bourgeoisie seeking refuge, once again, in natural law ideologies. In the first or so decade after the second world war[17], the so-called revival of natural law was at its highest. Yet it must be understood that this was not a resurrection of the natural law from a 'revolutionary angle'. Rather it was, and probably still is, an attempt to salvage positivism by modifying it with certain natural law elements. In both respects, the resultant amalgam was and is an ideology of the *status quo*. For instance, Fuller's 'internal morality of law'[18], the natural-law element in his positivism, is in sum nothing but an ideologised version of the various procedural rules against arbitrariness found and observed in Anglo-American jurisdictions.

Dworkin's and Rawl's attempts are of a similar genre. They may have resuscitated the 'social contract' and the 'original position' techniques of the philosophers of Enlightenment but have forcefully retained the positivist methodology of abstracting from state and society and asserting the primacy of law. Given the historical and social specificity of the present conjuncture, this amalgam has proved to be an ideal ideological defence of the *status quo,* promulgating welfarism at home and practising imperialism abroad. In an excellent critique of Rawl's *Theory of Justice,* Chattopadhyaya has pointed out that the individual contractarians in Rawl's 'original position' may not be 'Hobbesian savages nor Rousseauist angels' but are nonetheless Kantian ideal persons who do not exist in real-life situations where

> individuals are organized in different groups or classes and, as such, their demands for goods and plans of life prove considerably different, if not conflicting. Elements of difference and conflict are, in fact, accommodated or tolerated in the institutional arrangement and recognized from the Archemedean standpoint. That means that the scheme of cooperation envisaged in the original position seeks to legitimize social conflict and economic competition[19].

Chattopadhyaya has argued that Rawls has 'resorted to an abstractionist strategy without looking into diverse, puzzling, and interesting sociological contexts of justice that perhaps might threaten his 'clear and coherent geometry'. The only real society which apparently has weighed on his mind... is the American one'[20].

In this light, the post-World War II 'revival' of natural law was from its conservative angle to restore the ideological *status quo ante,* whose two major elements, on the international plane, were to roll back communism and prolong imperialism. The ideological myth that the Hitlerite Fascism was only an aberration, rather than inherent in the system of monopoly capitalism (i.e. imperialism), had to be given concrete expression; hence the UN Charter and the Universal Declaration of Human Rights, 1948. The international balance of forces at that time meant that the so-called Universal Declaration essentially embodied the Western conception of human rights. The ink on the Universal Declaration was hardly dry when the original rationale of both the revival of natural law as well as the Declaration was safely put away in the wardrobe of history as the Declaration was made an instrument in the cold war propaganda.

The revived natural law and the Declaration were presented as a counterweight to the strict positivism of essentially totalitarian states, a term which was now primarily applied to the socialist countries[21]. Indeed, since the Second World War, human rights-talk has become an important element in the ideological armoury of the Western countries on the international plane. We shall revert to this question in the next section. For the moment let us round up this discussion by emphasising some major imprints that positivism has left on the human rights discourse in Africa.

Positivism has strongly imparted its legalistic and formalistic characteristics to the human rights debate and activity in Africa. Besides the weak and defensive arguments of the cultural-relativists, African writers, particularly lawyers, have uncritically embraced the methodology of positivism and its prescriptions. Law is seen as a self-contained system of norms complete in itself, separate and abstracted from both state and society. The ills of society are seen as inconsistencies in the existing rules or lack of appropriate rules[22]. Therefore the tasks of the jurists become those of a technician, to formulate new norms and perfect the existing ones[23].

In the human rights field, this has found expression in two forms, both negative and positive. Negatively, human rights activity is presented essentially as non-ideological — relating to the basic humanity of every human being. Positively, the activity consists in standard-setting on the international plane and positivizing of these standards on the national plane. This in turn is reflected in the involvement of primarily two academic disciplines and professions in the human rights discourse — international law and international relations and their intellectual spokesperson, lawyers and diplomats (or political scientists American-style). Thus the whole debate that has taken place in the social sciences about inter-disciplinary approaches and the associated critique of the compartmentalisation of knowledge in the Western academia has by-passed the discourse in human rights.

Let us then sum-up our critique of the approaches and method implied in the prevailing human rights discourse by pointing out some of the more important ideological and political effects in so far as the African situation is concerned.

Firstly, we have noted at some length above that abstraction from social-history gives validity and credence both to the universalists and cultural-chauvinists. Indeed both sides in that debate are guilty of that abstraction. The broad sketch above has attempted to demonstrate that the concept of human rights has essentially been a very specific ideological construct invoked at various conjunctures in history.

Furthermore, we would submit, that if it has never been historically universal, much less has it been socially universal. Human rights ideology, in its different forms, has historically played a legitimising or mobilizing role in the struggle of classes to either rally for certain specific changes or to legitimise the status quo. And at no time, either philosophically or conceptually, has it applied to all human beings, for the very concept of 'human' has varied historically and socially. As Engels has succinctly observed:

> The justice of the Greeks and Romans held slavery to be just; the justice of the bourgeois of 1789 demanded the abolition of feudalism on the ground that it was unjust. For the Prussian Junker even the miserable District Ordinance is a violation of eternal justice. The conception of eternal justice, therefore, varies not only with time and place, but also with the persons concerned, and belongs among those things of which...'everyone understands something different'[24].

Secondly, as an ideology or ideologies, human rights conceptions have been part of a struggle in society. The second count on which the prevailing discourse is guilty is that it abstracts from these struggles and sees human rights as a kind of ideal or absolute standard to be attained and, in a typical Hegelian fashion, presents history as a veritable movement of ideas towards the perfection of human rights concepts and standards. This has grievous effects on even the practical activity of the so-called human rights activists. They substitute themselves as fighters for the people who then become, in their discourse, victims of human rights violations rather than being actors resisting these violations in the course of their struggle for emancipation[25].

Once, human rights conceptions are placed in their historical context, it is clearly seen that important historical declarations of rights were a kind of political manifesto of particular classes in the course of class struggle and they were all limited in life even if, during the dawn of capitalism, they were cast in the language of universalism which of course is the distinguishing hallmark of bourgeois 'juridical world outlook'[26] — universal in proclamation, particular in application.

Even the Universal Declaration of Human Rights and other UN Covenants can, by no means, be regarded as universal — the very debates challenging their universality prove this. Adamantia Pollis has pointed out:

> (These) different sets of rights stem from different conceptual frameworks. The Covenant on Social, Economic and Cultural Rights juxtaposed with the Universal Declaration clearly demonstrates the current polarization on the issue of human rights, a polarization rooted in different conceptions of the nature of persons, and of society,

> and of the relationship of one to the other. Western industrial countries espouse the priority of civil and political rights, while both the socialist and non-socialist Third World countries and the Eastern bloc countries argue the priority of economic and social rights[27].

Furthermore, both the prioritization debate and the dichotomy between the political/civil and social/economic rights stem from an idealist approach. The universalist position of course holds that all rights are integral and cannot be separated. But then what has come to be constituted as a catalogue of rights has always had historical and social specificity. Throughout the bourgeois era, the right to private property has occupied the central stage. From Locke's formulation of life, liberty and property expressed as inalienable rights, right through the Universal Declaration, it is the primacy of property rights which commanded centrality. Indeed, both life and liberty of millions of people (witness slavery, colonialism and plunder of the Third World) all over the world have been sacrificed at the altar of private property. Both the catalogue of rights as well as the centrality that certain rights come to occupy are a historically determined phenomenon.

Thirdly, the dichotomy between civil/political and social/economic rights itself is ideologically and politically charged. It is commonly said that while Western countries espouse the priority of civil/political rights, the Eastern bloc subscribes to the priority of social/economic rights. This division of rights has so much become part of the cold-war and imperialist propaganda that debaters have often overlooked the fact that the right to private property, so dear to the heart of the West, is an economic right.

Thus in the UN Declaration, which can be said to reflect largely the Western position, an economic right — the right to private property — occupies a place of pride while there is no mention whatsoever of one of the most important political rights, the right to self-determination. That, nonetheless, the priority debate rages on, demonstrates not only the ideological character of the human rights discourse but also its propaganda value internationally.

Fourthly, the prevailing human rights discourse on Africa has been singularly 'deficient' in contextualising the human rights ideology within the imperialist domination of Africa. Indeed, even the role of imperialism in the violation of human rights is hardly discussed in spite of the massive literature on human rights violations in Africa. To cite a quick example, in the dominant literature one again and again sees references to Bokassa, Amin and Nguema as gruesome perpetrators of human rights violations, which indeed they were; but these citings go without the mention of the fact that Bokassa was France's protege, that Nguema received support from Spain and the US[28] while Amin was installed by zionist Israel supported by Britain.

This 'omission' is so significant that we shall deal with it more broadly in the next section. Suffice it to mention, that even leading Africanists are quick to reproach African states of 'double standards'[29] for mild anti-colonial rhetoric in the United Nations, while reserving, at best, meaningless understatements for imperialist violations of human rights.

Finally, the individualist and ahistorical approach to human rights enables the dominant discourse to concentrate on episodes in their expository literature rather than focus on situations which give rise to these episodes[30]. The sum total of the above-mentioned 'biases' in the prevailing discourse, we would submit, amounts to the production and reproduction of a human rights ideology which objectively buttresses the imperialist oppression of Africa on the one hand, and the authoritarian/military domination of its people on the other.

IMPERIALISM AND HUMAN RIGHTS

In the preceding section we argued that the abstraction from social-history in the prevailing human rights discourse results in the fundamental failure to see 'human rights-talk' as historically and socially specific ideology with an important role in class struggles which underlie political standpoints and stances. This failure manifests itself most prominently in the African human rights discourse which is remarkable for its abstraction from the imperialist domination of Africa. And yet, in our opinion, it is precisely here that human rights talk expresses its ideological and political character in its sharpest forms.

Since the second world war, human rights talk has been one of the central planks in the foreign and domestic ideologies of the United States[31]. It is clearly expressed in the cold-war struggle with the Soviet bloc on the one hand, and in the oppression and domination of the Third World, including Africa, on the other. In some periods more intensely than others[32], the human rights ideology has been used by different regimes in the US on both these levels. In this regard it has played a double, if contradictory, role. On the international level, it is a rationalization for interference and intervention as well as domination of the Third World countries ('in the interest of democracy and free world') and on the domestic level it is an important element in reproducing the hegemony of imperial-bourgeois ideology by bolstering the image of the US as a country maintaining civilised human standards internationally[33].

This big-power chauvinism presented as 'international responsibility', has verged on almost fascist nationalism during times of conservative regimes like that of Reagan[34] as is conclusively demonstrated by incidents like the invasion of Grenada, the mining of Nicaragua's harbours and the bombing of Libya. This ideological human rights crusade has probably been effective in yet another respect, namely, in keeping out from the mainstream discourse (both analytical as well as expository) the active role of imperialism, particularly the US, in installing, supporting and aiding (including perfecting of the technological instruments of human rights violations from weapons of war to electric batons for torture)[35] Third World dictatorships and undemocratic regimes which have been among the greatest violators of human rights. The championing of human rights by the US has thus gone hand in hand with their violation. It follows that the human rights ideology has played the role of legitimising, or at least disguising, a contrary practice of imperialist powers.[36]

In a rare study linking human rights to US imperialism, Chomsky and Herman have shown that the US has consistently supported undemocratic dictatorships in the Third World. They have argued that there is almost a direct link between violations of human rights, US support in terms of economic investments and military aid. Giving figures, which we need not reproduce, the authors conclude:

> For most of the sample countries, U.S.-controlled aid has been positively related to investment climate and inversely related to the maintenance of a democratic order and human rights.[37].

The authors argue that US support for regimes known for systematic human rights violations is itself systematic and consistently tied to imperialist economic and strategic interests. '...US aid to terror-prone states ... *is positively related to terror and improvement of investment climate and negatively related to human rights...*'[38] The authors continue:

> The military juntas of Latin America and Asia are our juntas. Many of them were directly installed by us or are the beneficiaries of our direct intervention, and most of the others came into existence with our tacit support, using military equipment and training supplied by the United States. Our massive intervention and subversion over the past 25 years has been confined almost exclusively to overthrowing reformers, democrats, and radicals — we have rarely 'destabilized' right-wing military regimes no matter how corrupt or terroristic.[39]

This should not come as a surprise to any African who has the slightest knowledge of reality beyond the thin veneer of official imperialist 'brain washing'. Who does not know that Mobutu, who gracefully presides over death and detention chambers of Zaire, was installed by the CIA?[40] Who is so ignorant as to forget that the Lion of Juddah (Haile Selassie), who turned his country into a jungle where people in their thousands starved to death in fear and famine, was one of the greatest beneficiaries of US military arsenal? Many know that the US is one of the staunchest allies of South Africa; the military supplier of UNITA in Angola; the benefactor of dictators like Banda and Moi and the protector of Liberia's military nincompoop Samuel Doe[41].

On the one hand, these facts are so well-documented that they need no repetition, yet on the other hand they have been so successfully suppressed in the mainstream human rights scholarship that they need to be broadcast from roof-tops. Even more alarming for Africa is the fact that such a basic and absolutely central question should find no place in human rights discourse both from African and Africanist scholarship as well as among human rights activists and NGOs.

I suggested earlier that in that sense Chomsky's and Herman's work was exceptional. As a matter of fact so exceptional that undisguised attempts were made in the US to suppress it[42]. It has hardly received much notice in the liberal circles, including the Africanist champions of human rights in Africa. African scholars are guilty, even more so, in lending credence to this politically nihilist position on human rights. The furthest liberal Africanists allow themselves to go is an occasional indulgence in by-the-way understatements which tend to be positively misleading rather than illuminating. Listen to leading human rights activists, with interests in human rights issues in Africa and Asia:

> In almost all instances where authoritarian governments have come into existence in the Third World, they have sought to preserve a facade of democracy, usually retaining an atrophied and manipulated electoral process to present the appearance of a legitimate grounding on the consent of the governed. In some real but unquantifiable degree, this unhappy result has been caused by policies of the United States government which, as in Central and South America, have been satisfied by a minimal formalistic threshold, as a consequence of which de jure recognition and more material benefits have been readily granted to otherwise illegitimate regimes[43].

Placed beside the statements from Chomsky and Herman quoted above one cannot but be *pained* by such monumental understatement on the role of imperialism which has been 'the most important single instigator, administrator, and moral and material sustainer of serious bloodbaths in the years that followed World War II'[44]. And yet one of the same authors, correctly this time, can express her outrage in very strong terms when it comes to what she calls the 'double-standards' on human rights adopted by African states in the United Nations[45].

Another form of treatment of imperialism in the left-liberal Africanist writings on human rights is to place imperialist domination on the level of one of the external factors contributing to human rights abuses. Scoble formulates it as follows:

> The denials of peoples' rights in the Third World, including simply the failure to achieve them in any greater degree, have external causes. ...
>
> Even so, imagine the miraculous; let us suppose that a just New International Economic Order were to be achieved by tomorrow morning. Would there then be any warrant for assuming that denials and active violations of peoples' and human rights would disappear overnight as well? I think not. There are domestic causes as well, of which official corruption, nepotism, and governmental incompetence are probably only the most visible symptoms[46].

For us imperialism is neither external nor a factor or a cause[47]. And we do not consider the trade union demands of the essentially neo-colonial African states summed-up in the New International Economic Order as constituting the anti-imperialist, democratic standpoint of the African people. But let me not digress at this juncture.

Another typical example of such multi-causation, multi-factor explanations and methodology is to be found in the background paper prepared by Philip and Eide for an African Seminar on Human Rights and Development held at Gaborone in 1982. Disowning any ideological leanings or any particular philosophical approach, the background paper claims only to 'provide some information and raise a number of questions'. It warns its African participants:

> Do not expect full coherence in this presentation. Several different approaches to the problems here discussed are possible, coherence would mean that only one approach

> had been singled out to the detriment of others. That cannot be the purpose of a background discussion paper[48].

Indeed, that, we are incessantly reminded, is the role of expatriate experts in Africa, be they human right-ists, humanists, economists or agronomists!

Eclecticism, empiricism and multiplicity of causes and approaches as an explanation of course does not mean that the 'background paper' or the 'information' and 'issues' presented therein do not have ideological and philosophical coherence. Denial of ideological or philosophical approach is precisely what constitutes the outlook of the monopolist bourgeois and their academic spokesperson in the present era[49]. Not surprisingly, neither the background paper nor other papers in this important African seminar on human rights, except perhaps the speeches made by the representatives of the liberation movements, had anything consistent to say on the imperialist ideology of human rights, or at an empirical level, about violations of human rights by imperialism. Such a discussion presumably would have been too political and unacceptable on moral and juristic planes where the human rights discourse is located. Human rights are too noble to be politicised, it would seem.

The underdevelopment/structuralist approach adopted by leftist-liberals such as Rhoda Howard, to whom references have been made earlier in this work, is also not free of an eclectic view of imperialism. In her book-length study of human rights in nine Commonwealth African countries, Howard[50] nowhere develops a clear conception of imperialism. Her social-structural approach, as she calls it, allows her only to talk of classes but dismiss class struggle, by default so to speak, ending up in such pitfalls as proclaiming universality (presumably ideological too) of human rights; revolution (which type?) as not a 'realistic option' etc. That, given her approach, she fails to see the centrality of the right to self-determination is quite understandable.

Let us, however, not dwell further on the limitations of such an approach except to point out that it has no value even in exploring the possibility of appropriating the ideology of human rights for the working people in the course of their struggle for democracy. This critique will become clearer in the next chapter where we outline an alternative conceptualisation. Let us briefly examine another approach which, although not quite part of the mainstream, suffers from some serious problems.

Eze, an African scholar, has done a book-length[51] study of human rights in Africa. His approach is what would be conventionally regarded as 'Marxist-Leninist'. While Eze's historical and social treatment of human rights enables him to avoid the manifold pitfalls of cultural-relativists, liberals and left-liberals, it has thrown up another issue which African activists have to take account of seriously. It is clear from Eze's analysis that the 'Marxist-Leninist' approach he identifies with is the one propounded by the Soviet and East European 'socialist' countries.

Authors from these 'socialist' countries have of course arrogantly proclaimed that their brand is the only authentic version of Marxist-Leninist theory and practice[52]. However, their practice in Africa alone should make us wary of these claims[53]. For instance, their position on the right to self-determination, which for Africans, as we argue later, is the central right, has been anything but Marxist-Leninist. The Soviet revisionist theories on socialist-oriented states and the so-called non-capitalist countries[54], being the theoretical underpining for the achievement of certain foreign-policy aims, are a far-cry from Marxism and Leninism. Ideological-philosophical approaches and outlook are not perfected in specific geographical locations nor are they a monopoly of countries, whatever their historical antecedents and contemporary self-declarations. Rather, we would assert, Marxism-Leninism is class- and historical-specific and that is how Marxism should be seen and applied concretely in Africa.

Eze, despite the limitations mentioned, does develop a useful framework to understand the right to self-determination. Yet he does not apply this framework concretely in cases like that of Eritrea, for example. Secondly, because of the use of categories borrowed from Soviet versions of Marxism-Leninism, Eze fails to identify correctly the present stage of the revolution in Africa and the place of human rights ideology in it. Thus for him what we have in Africa are two types of states, capitalist- and socialist-oriented. Socialism and capitalism themselves are seen as 'options' open to Africa[55].

This way of conceptualising ideology is not only voluntaristic but runs against the very grain of Marxism-Leninism in which an ideology bears a class character and is not an item on a menu to be picked up by any class, country or state as and when it wishes. Similarly, Eze falls into the pitfall of eulogising one-party states in Africa because they are socialist-oriented or non-capitalist failing to see that as a matter of fact the one-party system in Africa has little to do with socialism but is rather an ideological fig-leaf to cover authoritarianism.[56].

Finally, Eze also fails to locate the class struggle correctly and what role, if any, human-rights ideology could play in advancing the struggle of the popular classes. The result is that the discussion of human rights becomes sterile for it is seen in the narrow terms of capitalist and socialist countries. Thus in one (capitalist) human rights are usually violated in spite of declarations, in the other (socialist) human rights are restricted, but correctly so, because material conditions do not exist for their complete fulfilment. Restrictions on rights in the 'socialist-oriented' African countries are justified presumably because the 'state of the masses' is making all efforts to develop productive forces and get rid of exploitative relations.

For Eze, the question of the promotion and protection of human rights becomes the business of the state. Even the question of socialism and capitalism becomes one of choice — presumably to be chosen by states. Therefore the role of masses on the one hand, and the role of human rights in the struggle of the popular classes on the other, finds no place in Eze's book in spite of its comprehensive treatment of the subject and its generally progressive inclinations.

THE 'HUMAN RIGHTS COMMUNITY'

What constitutes the 'human rights community'? These are the Western NGOs, scholars and human rights activists, a few African based NGOs, and intellectuals engaged in human rights discourse which we covered at great length in Chapter One. If the prevailing discourse abstracts from imperialism and class struggle, as I argued in the preceding section, human rights activities of both the Western and African NGOs similarly abstract from exposing violation of human rights by imperialism. Moreover, on the question of exposing the imperialist system, which creates and provides the soil for human rights violations, the mainstream human rights community continues to be evasive, if not apologetic.

Western NGOs and scholarship, no doubt, concentrate a lot of time and energy on exposing human rights violations in Africa by African states. In itself this is a useful activity, for publicity may hopefully, to whatever small extent, act as a deterrent to potential violators. But, since this is not done in the context of imperialism, this activity, we submit, objectively reproduces imperialist ideology of human rights. Omission here is as fatal as any commission could be. Pollis has correctly pointed out that 'Most Western-based human rights organizations are, to a greater or lesser degree, political advocates of the West, albeit unconsciously, and of the Western concept of human rights'[57].

Western Africanist scholarship, on the other hand, spends inordinate time refuting cultural-relativism of their African counterparts or denouncing the double-standards adopted by African governments in the UN and other forums. As was observed earlier, it is a testimony to this one-sided nature of human rights activity that we came across only one book-length study relating imperialism to human rights in which the role of US imperialism in violating and creating conditions for the violation of human rights in Africa and other Third World countries is unequivocally exposed. It is precisely this study which has found little response in the Western scholarship on human rights. Chomsky and Herman have this to say on what should be the responsibility of Western intellectuals in this regard.

> For privileged Western intellectuals, the proper focus for their protest is at home. The primary responsibility of US citizens concerned with human rights today is on the continuing crimes of the United States: the support for terror and oppression in large parts of the world, the refusal to offer reparations or aid to the recent victims of US violence. Similar considerations apply elsewhere. French intellectuals may, if they choose, devote their energies to joining the chorus of protest against Cambodian atrocities that has been conducted by the international press (including the *New York Times*, the Soviet press, indeed virtually every articulate segment in the industrial societies). As long as such protest is honest and accurate — often it is not, as we shall see — it is legitimate, though further questions may be raised about its impact. This small increment to the international barrage on Cambodia had little if any effect in mitigating harsh practices there, though it had a powerful effect on ideological renewal in the West and help prepare the ground for the Vietnamese invasion of Cambodia in January 1979. These effects were predictable, and predicted. French intellectuals interested in doing something to alleviate suffering in Southeast Asia where their impact might be positive would have been better advised to expend their efforts in protesting the announcement by their government that it proposes to join in the glorious massacre in East Timor by supplying arms, setting up an arms industry and providing diplomatic cover for Indonesia[58].

The above, *mutatis mutandis*, applies to Africanists as well. Thus what Western intellectuals say about violations in Uganda, Zaire, Equatorial Guinea etc. may be true but, to use Chomsky and Herman once again, 'it reeks of hypocrisy and opportunism'[59] when the role of Britain and Israel in installing Idi Amin, the role of the CIA in identifying and installing Mobutu, the role of Spain, US and France, and even the Soviet Union in Equatorial Guinea etc. is rarely mentioned or, if mentioned, is glossed over.

Even worse, the same 'hypocrisy and opportunism' is reproduced within the African scholarship and activity on human rights. The few African NGOs, funded as they are by their Western counter-parts or other Western funding agencies, rarely touch on the role of imperialism. They do not even expose the crimes of their own states. Instead much time is spent on refining legal concepts of human rights and the machinery for implementation. As we noted earlier, the so-called human rights activity in Africa has been largely dominated by lawyers. Thus even the developments of other social sciences have by-passed them. African NGOs that are set up, it would seem, are institutional mechanisms by which to obtain foreign funds: they are, what might be called, FFUNGOs (foreign funded NGOs) rather than grass-root organisations of the intellectuals and the people to struggle for rights.

At best these FFUNGOs of the 'intellectuals' see themselves as a kind of think-tanks to research and churn out policy recommendations for states, the very violators of human rights. Their approach to human rights work is thus dictated by these primary objectives. They specialise in organising pan-African conferences where intellectuals meet; present and listen to the usual legalistic papers on rights; fight over positions and end up holding parties where the funding agencies are graciously thanked and invited to donate more. There is little, if any, serious collective reflection on the situations in their own countries, or on the imperialist domination of the continent. Discussions on possibilities of organising grass-root people's organisations and inventing new methods of waging democratic struggles would be considered odious at such gatherings.

This is in sharp contrast, for example, to the approaches of some Asian NGOs where there is an increasing tendency, firstly, to concentrate on organising genuine people's NGOs (as opposed to GONGOs, i.e. government organised NGOs) which, secondly, would be involved in grass-roots work and, thirdly, consciously distance themselves from imperialist ideology and the human rights crimes of their compradorial ruling classes.[60]. I will revert to this issue in the chapter on reconceptualisation.

What then is the objective effect, good intentions notwithstanding, of the human rights activity and scholarship that we have just summarised? It seems to me this immediately brings in the role of intellectuals, both Africanists and Africans, in the present era of imperialist domination of Africa and the authoritarian compradorial states.

In this regard, I can do no better than refer to an excellent piece by George Lukacs 'On the Responsibility of Intellectuals'[61] written a generation ago but even more valid today. In that piece, Lukacs argued that the elements of Hitler's fascist ideology were already present in the theoretical writings of the intellectual giants of the day. In other words, intellectuals were partly responsible for the crimes of Hitler by developing — consciously or unconsciously — the ideologies used by Hitler to mobilise the people in his support.

Lukacs goes on to warn his contemporaries of providing an ideological garb for imperialism which could easily slip into a new form of fascism. This, he calls, nihilist hypocrisy.

> This new stage in the development of imperialism will quite probably not be called fascism. And concealed behind the new nomenclature lies a new ideological problem: the 'hungry' imperialism of the Germans brought forth a nihilistic cynicism which openly broke with all traditions of humanity. The fascist tendencies arising today in the U.S.A. work with the method of a nihilistic hypocrisy. They carry out the suppression and exploitation of the masses in the name of humanity and culture.
>
> Let us look at an example. It was necessary for Hitler, supported by Gobineau and Chamberlain, to formulate a special theory of races in order to mobilize demagogically his masses for the extermination of democracy and progress, humanism and culture. The imperialists of the U.S.A. have it easier. They need only universalize and systematize their old practices concerning the Negroes. And since these practices have up to now been 'reconcilable' with the ideology portraying the U.S.A. as a champion of democracy and humanism, there can be no reason why such a *Weltanschauung* of nihilist hypocrisy could not arise there, which by demagogic means, could become dominant.[62]

Lukacs argues that nihilist hypocrisy manifests itself in fetishization of phenomena without investigating their real social and historical content. 'Today it is in the life interests of the imperialist bourgeoisie to annihilate the capability for social-historical orientation among the intelligentsia'[63]. This, as we have seen, is richly illustrated by the prevailing human rights discourse.

For the African scholar and intellectual, particularly the one who sees himself as a human rights activist, the responsibility is even greater. Yet he seems to have woefully failed in this regard. The cultural-relativist argument has provided the likes of Mobutu and Banda with the ideological weapons of 'authenticity' and 'traditionalism' to eliminate basic democracy. The 'ideology of developmentalism'[64] (development before democracy) has been abundantly used to create authoritarian monstrosities called one-party states. And now, both terror and suppression of the rights of people is rationalised by military juntas in the name of socialist-orientation and non-capitalist development.

For the latter, Soviet revisionists have gratuitously provided both the theory and the weapons of suppression from Uganda[65] to Ethiopia[66]. Like Lukacs, Paulin Hountondji warns his fellow African intellectuals to beware of ideologies which only rationalise repression.

> In Africa now the individual must liberate himself from the weight of the past as well as from the allure of ideological fashions. Amid the diverse but, deep down, so strangely similar catechisms of conventional nationalism and of equally conventional pseudo-Marxism, amid so many state ideologies functioning in the Fascist mode, deceptive alibis behind which the powers that be can quietly do the opposite of what they say and say the opposite of what they do, amid this immense confusion in which the most vulgar police state pompously declares itself to be a 'dictatorship of the proletariat' and neo-fascists mouthing pseudo-revolutionary platitudes called 'Marxist-Leninists', reducing the enormous theoretical and political subversive power of Marxism to the dimensions of a truncheon, in which, in the name of revolution, they kill, massacre, torture the workers, the trade unionists, the executives, the students: in the midst of all this intellectual and political bedlam we must all open our eyes wide and clear our own path. Nothing less will make discussions between free and intellectually responsible individuals possible[67].

In sum then, it may be said that in this 'scenario' of human rights scholarship and activity the dramatis personae on the human rights stage are competent jurists and skilful diplomats with the 'grass-root' support of Western do-gooders whereas the African people pale into periphery as helpless victims, while the curtain remains drawn on imperialism (which we know calls the shots from behind the stage) as the African states and ruling classes play the master of ceremonies.

NOTES

1. Alan S. Rosenbaum (ed.), *op.cit.*, p.9.
2. Zoltan Peteri, 'Citizens Rights and the Natural Law Theory', in Szabo (ed.), *Socialist Conception*, pp.83-119 at p.86.
3. Rhoda, *Human Rights*, *op.cit.*, p.218. For a paternalistic and singularly arrogant formulation of this position see MacDermot quoted in Richardson, *op.cit.*, p.40. He says:

   > What the Western countries have given to the world in recent times is this monster, the nation-state. We have a tremendous concentration of power in the central government, and we have created states, where there aren't even nations in many parts of the world, armed with these powers. And unless these states are going to be utterly arbitrary in their rule, they've got to operate under a rule or system of law. Consequently, every state in the world now has a system of law which is based on what are fundamentally Western concepts of law, because these concepts ...developed as part of the nation-state.
   >
   > So, consequently, when we are — as we are constantly — fighting and struggling to assist lawyers and others in these (new) countries to erect a structure of the rule of law, we are only giving them, as it were, the rest of the package — namely, the machinery by which the citizen is protected from the abuse of power by this potentially horrific mechanism.
4. *Ibid.*, p.224.
5. Szabo, 'Foundations', *op.cit.*
6. Frederick Engels, *The Housing Question* in Marx & Engels, *Selected Works*, vol.2 (Moscow: Progress Publishers, 1969), p.365.
7. See Lloyd, *op.cit.*, p.79.
8. *Ibid.*, p.83.
9. See Richardson, *op.cit.*, p.5; Rosenbaum, *op.cit.*, p.2 and Lloyd *op.cit.*
10. Pollis, *op.cit.*, p.7. 'The notion of man as an autonomous, rational, calculating being has been exactly that: a notion of man but not of woman, and not even all men but only of some'.
11. When the European Convention of 4 November 1950 was being negotiated, its Article 53 excluded the non-metropolitan countries which led Senghor, the then deputy in the French Parliament, to caution them lest they prepare a Declaration of the Rights of 'the European Man'. That is exactly what they did. See M'Baye, 'OAU', *op.cit.*, p.583.
12. See E. B. Pashukanis, *Law and Marxism: A General Theory* (London: Ink/Links, 1978) and I.D. Balbus, 'Commodity Form and Legal Form: An Essay on the 'Relative Autonomy' of the Law', *Law and Society*, Winter 1977.
13. Marx, *The Civil War* in *France in Selected Works*, vol.II *op.cit.*, p. 178. V.I.Lenin, *Imperialism, the Highest Stage of Capitalism* in *Collected Works*, vol.22 (Moscow: Progress Publishers, 1964.).
14. Quoted in Lloyd, *op.cit.*, p.304.
15. *Op.cit.*
16. See Issa G. Shivji, 'Notes on the Status of Legal Rights in Tanzania; A Jurisprudential Treatment', paper presented to the Silver Jubilee Seminar of the Faculty of Law, University of Dar-es-Salaam, October, 1986 (mimeo.).
17. V. Tumanov, *Contemporary Bourgeois Legal Thought*, (Moscow: Progress Publishers, 1979), p.268.

18. L.L. Fuller, *The Morality of Law*, extract in Lloyd, *op.cit.*, pp.148-54.
19. Chattopadhyaya, *op.cit.*, p.180.
20. *Ibid.*, p.183.
21. Tumanov., *op.cit.*,
22. Immediately after independence, American lecturers were trotting around African University campuses selling their 'Law and Development' courses in which they preached that development could be enhanced, facilitated, encouraged etc. through law.
23. See Issa G. Shivji, *Law, State and the Working Class in Tanzania* (London: James Currie, 1986), 'Introduction'.
24. Engels, *Anti-duhring*, in Marx, Engels & Lenin *On Historical Materialism* (Moscow: Progress Publishers, 1972), p.205.
25. We do not believe that there is a kind of inevitable emancipation as an ultimate idyll; rather emancipation itself is a historically relative goal.
26. This is Engels' phrase quoted in V. A. Tumanov, *op.cit.*, ch.1.
27. Pollis quoted in Richardson, *op.cit.*, p.19.
28. See Fegley, *op.cit.*, p.41. The Soviet Union too had relations with Equatorial Guinea including unlimited fishing rights in its waters while Continental Oil and Standard Oil had offshore exploration rights.
29. See Laurie S. Wiseberg, 'Human Rights in Africa: Toward a definition of the problem of double-standard', in *Issue: A Quarterly Journal of the Africanist Opinion* vi, no.4:3-13 (Winter, 1976).
30. This distinction is discussed by Alvaro Bunster, 'Human rights: Bases for a new system of safeguard', *IFDA DOSSIER* 20, Nov./Dec. 1980, pp.81-94.
31. See David P. Forsythe, 'Human Rights in US Foreign Policy: Retrospect and Prospect', paper prepared for the Foreign Policy Research Seminar, Columbia University, Center for the Study of Human Rights, September, 21, 1987.
32. Compare the Carter with Reagan eras, for instance. See in this regard A. L. Jinadu, *Human Rights and US-African Policy under President Carter* (Lagos: Nigerian Institute of International Affairs, 1980). See also Richard A. Falk, 'Superpower Intervention in the Third World: the US case', in *IFDA Dossier*, No. 42, (July/August, 1984), pp.45-55.
33. Richard Falk, 'The Algiers Declaration of the Rights of Peoples and the Struggle for Human Rights', in Antonio Cassese (ed.), *U.N. Law/Fundamental Rights: Two Topics in International Law* (The Netherlands: Sijthoff & Noordhoff, 1979), p.227.
34. For aspects of Reagan's African policy see Mohamed A. El-Khawas, 'Reagan's African Policy: A Turn to the Right', *A Current Bibliography on African Affairs* 16, No.3:207-26 (1983-4).
35. '...Rather than standing in detached judgment over the spread of repression abroad, the United States stands at the supply end of a pipeline of repressive technology extending to many of the world's authoritarian governments. And despite everything this administration has said about human rights, there is no evidence that this pipeline is being dismantled. In fact, its relative durability suggests that the delivery of repressive technology to authoritarian regimes abroad is a consistent and international product of our foreign policy, rather than a peripheral or accidental one'. Michael Klare, *Supplying Repression*, Field Foundation, December, 1977, p.10, quoted in Noam Chomsky and Edward S. Herman, *The Washington Connection and Third World Fascism: The Political Economy of Human Rights* — vol.1 (Boston: South End Press, 1979), p.46.
36. As a matter of fact, even on the level of international human rights regime, the US has dragged its feet. It was not particularly enthusiastic about the UN Declaration; has not yet ratified the International Covenants (1966) and opposed provisions

of the Inter-American Convention on enforcement of rights which, it argued, would derogate from its state sovereignty, for a whole decade. See Claude E. Welch, 'The OAU and Human Rights: Towards a New definition', *Journal of Modern African Studies* 19, no.3:401-420 (1981). This in addition to the well-known support that the US gives to various dictatorial regimes in the UN from Argentina, Chile, Israel, to Zaire.

37. Chomsky & Herman, *op.cit.*, p.8.
38. *Ibid.*, p.16.
39. Ibid.
40. There is considerable literature on this. But see Nzongola-Ntalaja, 'The Second Independence Movement in Congo-Kinshasa', in Peter Anyang' Nyong'o (ed.), *Popular Struggles for Democracy in Africa* (London: UNU/Zed Books, 1987), pp.13-36.
41. For US support of Liberia from the True Whig governments to Doe see Peter A. Nyong'o, 'Popular Alliances and the State in Liberia, 1980-85', in Nyong'o (ed.), *op.cit.*, pp.209-26. Even the American Lawyers Committee for Human Rights Report on Liberia devotes some 10 pages of its 176 to 'The Role of the US'. That this is done in a typically paternalistic fashion where US is impliedly urged to save Liberia for democracy is characteristic of all such 'liberal' positions. If the US government sees itself as a policeman of the world, some of its human rights activists see their government as a 'saviour of democracy'. These positions are two sides of the same coin, 'imperialist pragmatism'. What else can one make of the following conclusion in the Committee's Report:

    > Most Liberians still look to America as an agent of democracy and human rights. *Few if any have shown an inclination to look elsewhere, yet.* There is no armed insurgency in Liberia, nor any external military threat. Most of the victims of abuses described in this report are scholars and journalists and businessmen and women; *they have no sinister designs. They pose no threat to American interests.* Their successors may not be so patient.

    Liberia: *A Promise Betrayed*, op.cit., p.6.
42. See fn.44.
43. Scoble & Wiseberg, *Access to Justice, op.cit.*, p.124.
44. Chomsky & Herman, *op.cit.*, p.xiv. The italicised phraseology in this sentence in the text is suggested by a passage in Chomsky & Herman where they are narrating the suppression of the publication of their original monograph by the Warner communications and entertainment conglomerate whose subsidiary had contracted to publish the said monograph. The passage runs.

    > Mr. William Sarnoff, a high officer of the parent company, for example, was deeply pained by our statement on page 7 of the original that 'the leadership in the United States, as a result of its dominant position and wide-ranging counter-revolutionary efforts, has been the most important single instigator, administrator, and moral and material sustainer of serious bloodbaths in the years that followed World War II'. So pained were Sarnoff and his business associates, in fact, that they were quite prepared to violate a contractual obligation in order to assure that no such material would see the light of day? *Ibid.*
45. Wiseberg, 'Double Standards', *Op. cit.*
46. Scoble, 'NGOs', *op.cit.*, p.199.
47. For a discussion of this see the Introduction, *supra.*
48. Gaborone Seminar, *op.cit.*, p.1.
49. Underlying American scholarship at the present times is philosophical pragmatism

a là W.James and political empiricism.

50. Rhoda Howard, *Human Rights op.cit.*
51. *Human Rights in Africa: Some Selected Problems op.cit.*
52. Szabo, 'Foundations', *op.cit.*, p.36.

    ...the only course to be accepted as the socialist course is the one based on the teachings of Marx. Undoubtedly, it is in the socialist countries that these have widened into a socially recognised trend: therefore, in our opinion, the theory, as professed there, should be accepted as an authentic interpretation.
53. See, *inter alia,* Lucas Khamis, *Imperialism To-Day* (Dar es Salaam: Tanzania Publishing House, 1981).
54. For the views of Soviet theorists see V. Chirkin & Yu. Yudin, *A Socialist-oriented State (Moscow: Progress Publishers, 1983).* It seems to me that the theories of socialist-orientation, which incidentally only apply to the Third World, is directly connected with the theory of the 'state of the whole people' which was made the cornerstone of the 1961 Programme of the Communist Party of the Soviet Union and which was one of the main bones of contention in the famous debate between the CPSU and the Chinese Communist Party. For the debate see CPC, *The Polemic on the General Line of the International Communist Movement* (London: Red Star Press, 1976). For the discussion of some African versions of this position see Issa G. Shivji, 'The State in the Dominated Social Formations of Africa: Some Theoretical Issues', *International Social Science Journal* 32, no.4, pp.730-42.
55. *Op.cit.*, p.5.
56. Holding out Tanzania as a successful example of a one-party state Eze surmises:

    A well-structured one-party state, with a political party based on mass participation and support, and that has jettisoned the capitalistic philosophy of government for a socialist-oriented philosophy and organisational structure, does, it is submitted, represent the real alternative for African countries. Ibid, p.59.

    Leaving aside the theoretical confusion in this statement, it is not even a correct empirical observation of 'real Africa'. His one-party states, including Congo-Brazaville and Tanzania which he mentions among others, have all been shown to be firmly located within neo-colonial social formations and authoritarian political systems. See Issa G. Shivji (ed.) *The State and the Working People in Tanzania* (Dakar: CODESRIA, 1986) and E. Wamba-dia-Wamba, 'The Experience of Struggle in the People's Republic of Congo', in Nyong'o, *op.cit.*, pp.96-110. This way of conceptualising the reality in Africa leads Eze to a dangerous position of even justifying the suppression of the organisational autonomy of the working people. For example, he argues that in the capitalist-oriented African states trade unions may be justified in fighting for higher wages etc., but in the socialist-oriented states there is no contradiction between them and the government and therefore they should assist in formulating socialist policies, Ibid., pp.61-2. See also below Chapters 3 & 4.
57. Richardson, *op.cit.*, p. 20.
58. *Op.cit.*, pp.38-9.
59. *Ibid.*, p.39.
60. There has been some interesting debate in India on the role of NGOs; their relation with imperialism and the local states. See Rajni Khothari, 'NGOs, the State and World Capitalism', *Economic and Political Weekly* XXI, no.50:2177-82 (December 13, 1986) In Asia, it seems, there are at least some critical positions towards FFUNGOs. For instance, the workshop entitled 'Access to Justice' organised by the US-based Human Rights Internet and the International Human

Rights Law Group, Washington, in Tagaytay, Phillipines, was not attended by some Asian groups partly because the funds came from the U.S. government — the same source which was then heavily arming the dictator Marcos. Such attitude is almost unheard of in Africa! See Scoble & Wiseberg, *Access to Justice, op.cit.*, pp.xi-xiii.

61. George Lukacs, 'On the Responsibility of Intellectuals', in Lukacs, *Marxism and Human Liberation* (New York: Dell Publishing, 1973) pp.267-277.
62. *Ibid.*, pp.270-1.
63. *Ibid.*, p.275.
64. For some discussion of this ideology see Shivji, 'Introduction', in Shivji,(ed.), *The State and the Working People op.cit.* And below, Chapters 3 & 4.
65. For the role of the Soviet Union in supplying arms to Idi Amin see Mahmood Mamdani, *Imperialism and Fascism in Uganda* (London: Heinemann, 1983).
66. For the Eritrean struggle see B. Habte Selassie, *Conflict and Intervention in the Horn* (New York: Monthly Review Press, 1980). For a mindless glorification of Mengistu's 'red terror' as revolutionary violence see Peter Schwab, 'The Response of the Left to Violence and Human Rights 'Abuses' in the Ethiopian Revolution', in Peter Schwab & Adamantia Pollis (eds.) *Towards a Human Rights Framework* (New York: Praegar, 1982), pp.189-201.
67. Paulin Hountondji, *op.cit.*, p.69.

3. REVOLUTIONISING HUMAN RIGHTS FRAMEWORK

RE-CONCEPTUALISATION

The discussion of the prevailing human rights discourse in Chapter One and its critique in Chapter Two have sufficiently exposed the need to build a new perspective on human rights in Africa. While this reconceptualisation is obviously a process involving constant interaction between the struggles of the African people and activists and, whereas no full-blown perspective can be built at a stroke, I believe the critique provides some elements or building blocks for beginning to erect a new perspective. In this Chapter therefore an attempt is made to thread together these elements with a view to open a debate on the reconceptualisation of human rights in Africa.

First, it is clear that human rights-talk should be historically situated and socially specific. For the African perspective this ought to be done frankly without being apologetic. Any debate conducted on the level of moral absolutes or universal humanity is not only fruitless but ideologically subversive of the interests of the African masses.

Historically, we should examine and define, albeit in broad terms, the present conjuncture in the transformation of Africa. Needless to say, this is a concrete task which may differ in each African country yet, it is submitted that it is possible to talk at the pan-African level on a certain level of generality. In the social sciences, there have been protracted debates on the issue. Here we only borrow some of their tentative conclusions without much argumentation. It is generally recognised that imperialist domination of Africa, from colonial to neo-colonial forms, constitutes the main point of departure for understanding the conditions of the African masses. However, this domination is not seen as an external factor but is rather built-in the relations that obtain within the political economy of Africa.

Imperialism allies with the most backward domestic forces, both traditional and modern, to maintain its stranglehold. Therefore within each of our social formations there are those social groups and forces that provide the social basis for imperialism and these are what we call compradorial forces. At the same time, it has to be clearly understood, theoretically as well as historically, that imperialism is a negation of all freedom, of all democracy. As Lenin said 'imperialism is indisputably the 'negation' of democracy in general, of all democracy'[1]. In Africa this has been proved true to the hilt as we have seen that most authoritarian regimes and military dictatorships derive their support from imperialism[2]. Therefore the present stage of the revolution in Africa is defined essentially as an anti-imperialist, democratic revolution or a National Democratic Revolution as discussed in the Introduction.

Socially too we have to identify specifically those social classes and groups in society who suffer oppression and exploitation under the neo-colonial situation and therefore who form the motive force of an anti-imperialist, democratic revolution. In Europe, democracy was the battle-cry of the rising bourgeoisie. In Africa today, by and large, such a bourgeoisie virtually does not exist. The African bourgeoisie is strategically compromised with imperialism to the extent that it cannot head even a democratic revolution. Hence the task of an anti-imperialist, democratic revolution falls largely on the shoulders of the working people. (This is what is new or national in the new or national democracy.)

Who are then the working people or the 'people'? This too is a concrete task but broadly all those social forces which at any particular time do not form part of the compradorial bloc, as defined above, constitute the 'people' whose core in Africa are workers, peasants, craftsmen, artisans and other similarly situated self-employed. Thus even the category of 'people' is historically defined and socially specific.

We therefore arrive at the first important building-block of the new perspective on human rights in Africa. It must be thoroughly anti-imperialist, thoroughly democratic and unreservedly in the interest of the 'people'.

Secondly, human rights, as we have seen, is an ideology. It ideologises certain social interests in the course of class struggles. And it plays either a legitimising role or a mobilising one. For the new perspective, the human rights ideology has to be appropriated in the interest of the people to play a mobilising role in their struggle against imperialism and compradorial classes and their state.

Therefore the new perspective must distance itself openly from imperialist ideology of human rights at the international level and cultural-chauvinist/developmentalist ideology of the compradorial classes, at the national level[3]. This is the second element or building-block in the new perspective.

Thirdly, the historical, social and ideological perspective suggested above at once generates a new conceptualisation of an 'human rights' ideology at a theoretical level. The new conceptualisation must clearly break from both the metaphysics of natural law as well as the logical formalism and legalism of positive law. It must be rooted in the perspective of class struggle. This means, first, that counter-posed to the individualist/liberal paradigm must be the collectivist/revolutionary conception. The right-holder, if you like, is not exclusively an autonomous individual but a collective: a people, a nation, a nationality, a national group, an interest/social group, a cultural/oppressed minority, etc. But this notion of 'collective' must be clearly distinguished from a fascist concept where the 'collective' is expressed in the oppressor state or a revisionist-'marxist' concept where both the 'collective' and the state cease to bear any class character[4].

Secondly, here right is not theorised simply as a legal right, which implies both a static and an absolutist paradigm, in the sense of an entitlement or a claim, but a means of struggle. In that sense it is akin to righteousness rather than right. Seen as a means of struggle, 'right' is therefore not a standard granted as charity from above but a standard-bearer around which people rally for struggle from below. By the same token, the correlate of 'right' is not duty (in the Hohfeldian sense) where duty-holders are identified and held legally or morally responsible but rather the correlate is power/privilege where those who enjoy such power/privilege are the subject of being exposed and struggled against.

Thirdly, therefore, the human rights vocabulary too undergoes transformation. In the new perspective one does not simply sympathise with the 'victims' of human rights violations and beg the 'violators' to mend their ways in numerous catalogued episodes of violations; rather one joins the oppressed/exploited/dominated or ruled against the oppressors/exploiters/dominant and ruling to expose and resist, with a view ultimately to overcome, the situation which generates human rights violations.

Finally, the new perspective lends a totally different meaning to the prioritization debate as well as a new content and form to human rights activity and community. These we discuss in the next sections of this Chapter.

Before we proceed, it has to be made clear lest it is misunderstood, that what is being suggested for the new perspective is an ideological and theoretical break with the dominant discourse on human rights. This does not of course mean that certain elements from the old perspective cannot be fruitfully integrated in the new one. Indeed, in that sense, our suggested building blocks are a series of shifts in *biases* which hopefully will generate a new perspective. To put it another way, the new always partakes of what is good and meritorious in the old. Neither social transformations nor ideological breaks in that sense begin from a clean slate.

CENTRALITY OF RIGHTS: RIGHT TO SELF-DETERMINATION AND RIGHT TO ORGANISE

The prioritization debate and the way it is presented in the prevailing discourse, it is submitted, is fundamentally flawed. So also is the apparent answer to it in the form of 'integrated' or 'comprehensive' approach or the so-called 'basic needs' approach. The major characteristic of these positions is that they do not see human rights as an ideology of struggle but a collection of either moral or legal values/norms to be attained.

In the light of the aforementioned argument, it is clear that throughout there has been no such thing as 'integrated' rights. Rather there have always been certain rights which have occupied the central place and attention. In the heyday of bourgeois era, for instance, the right to private property was central. In that sense it took priority over other rights including life and liberty. In the present African conjuncture, it is submitted that the *central** rights are 'right to self-determination' and the 'right to organise'. Both these rights appear in the traditional catalogue of human rights.

The rest of this section will be devoted to elaborate on these rights and justify as to why they are central in the present stage of the African revolution.

Right to self-determination

The 'right to self-determination' is eminently a democratic right or principle. It first arose during the bourgeois democratic revolutions in the 18th and 19th century Europe. Its comprehensive theorisation is to be found in Lenin's writings where it was elaborated as 'Right of Nations to Self-Determination'. The Soviet State was the first to

* These rights are *central* but not *exclusive*. A cluster of rights connected with the integrity and security of a person — life, liberty and various freedoms — still remain very important and are in no way meant to be undermined. For an interface between individual personal rights and collective rights see my discussion in 'State and Constitutionalism in Africa: A New Democratic Perspective', Keynote Paper delivered at the African Regional Institute on Comparative Constitutionalism, Harare, May 22-25, 1989.

put it into practice when in the Declaration of Rights of the Working and Exploited People it proclaimed complete independence of Finland, evacuation of troops from Persia and freedom of self-determination for Armenia[5]. In the League of Nations, it was not yet recognized as a principle of international law.[6]. It was for the first time included in the United Nations Charter at the insistence of the Soviet Union, albeit in a truncated form[7]. Significantly, it does not appear in the Universal Declaration of Human Rights and did not find a clearer formulation until 1966 in the International Covenants[8].

The principle of self-determination, or as it has been now formulated, 'right of people to self-determination', is now generally recognised as a right in international law.[9]. What is contentious is of course what it implies, includes and excludes. We briefly look at that debate.

In Lenin's thesis on the 'Right of Nations to Self-determination', it is very clear that he was referring to the right of oppressed nations to independence and formation of their own separate states. Hence there the right includes the right to secede.[10]. In the *Decree on Peace* which was written by Lenin, he gave a definition of annexation which also serves very well as a definition of self-determination for annexation is nothing but a 'violation of the self-determination of a nation'[11]. Lenin characterised annexation as:

> any incorporation of a small or weak nation into a large or powerful state without the precisely, clearly and voluntarily expressed consent and wish of that nation, irrespective of the time when such forcible incorporation took place, irrespective also of the degree of development or backwardness of the nation forcibly annexed to the given state, or forcibly retained within its borders, and irrespective, finally, of whether this nation is in Europe or in distant overseas countries[12].

Since the Second World War and during the era of decolonisation, the Soviet practice has consistently applied only one aspect of Lenin's thesis, i.e. formation of sovereign states by the formerly colonised people but it has otherwise resolutely upheld the principle of territorial integrity, state sovereignty and non-intervention. In Lenin, it is clear, that the principle applied not only to colonial nations 'in distant overseas countries' but also to nations in independent states such as in Europe.

Secondly, the Soviet practice has been that the principle is implemented once a colonised country gains independence while for

Lenin it was a continuing principle and could be invoked at any time by an oppressed nation even in a sovereign state.[13].

The Soviet practice is akin to the UN, the OAU and the Afro-Asian state practice. In its own relations with African states, the USSR has applied that position even in opposition to a struggle for national self-determination as in Eritrea.[14]. As Cassese puts it succinctly:

> According to socialist countries, self-determination, considered as the right to non-intervention, means the right that foreign States shall not interfere in the life of the community against the will of the government. It does not include the right that a foreign state shall not interfere in the life of the community against the interests of the population but at the request or at any rate with the tacit approval of the government.[15].

What has been stated by Cassese was best illustrated in the case of Idi Amin's Uganda where the Soviet Union supplied that fascist dictator with arms to slaughter the population[16].

Restriction of right to self-determination to colonial and colonial-like situations (South Africa) in the state practice of the Soviet Union and the Afro-Asian countries and the absolutising of the principle of territorial integrity is based on two-fold rationale. On the one hand there is the fear that the recognition of this right would lead to dismemberment of states and encouragement of secessionist movements and on the other it will provide a fertile ground to foreign powers to support such movements thereby weakening the sovereignty of the African states. Of course, underlying both these 'reasons' are the very nature of the African states which have failed to apply both consistent anti-imperialism and democracy. Recognition of the right to secede does not automatically mean that every nation or people have a duty to secede; indeed the fathers of this right believed that the very recognition of the right to secede and democratic treatment of all nations and nationalities within a particular state lead to a situation of voluntary union of nations rather than secession. For, to emphasise once again, the right belongs to an oppressed nation and if a nation is not oppressed, that is to say, it is treated democratically and accorded equality, both the reason and rationale for secession disappear.

The problem in Africa has been precisely that the existing states have not treated nations and nationalities under them democratically; hence their fear that the recognition of this 'right' will lead to secession. As a matter of fact, oppression of nations and nationalities in Africa have led to devastating civil wars and gross violations of the rights of the whole masses of people[17].

A very good illustration in this regard is the case of Sudan. The central problems of the Sudan and the causes underlying the present war have been well-summed up by Akol as: 'the dominance of one nationality over the others, the sectarian and religious bigotry that has dominated the Sudanese political scene since independence, and the unequal development in the country'[18]. In other words, Akol has identified precisely the factors — national oppression, undemocratic, authoritarian state system, and imperialist domination — which are supposed to be countered by the principle and concept of self-determination. The history of Sudan itself illustrates these tensions and the fact that their relative resolution is intricately tied up with these factors.

The only time Sudan had 'peace', so far as the question of Southern Sudan is concerned, was after the signing of the Addis Ababa agreement in 1972[19]. The agreement provided for a fairly comprehensive self-government for Southern Sudan. And during the first period of the operation of the agreement some intention was shown to redress extreme underdevelopment in the South[20]. But the irony of the agreement was that while Southern Sudan was granted certain democratic rights, the central government continued to be run on the basis of Nimeiry's authoritarian state and party structures. It is doubtful if even the original signing of the agreement was based on a principled stand or simply an expediency for Nimeiry to survive.

With the benefit of the hindsight, it is not far-fetched to say that it was expediency[21]. Over the next ten years Nimeiry gradually made inroads into the agreement and finally abrogated it in June 1983 and, among other things, imposed Shari'ah law contrary to the 1973 Constitution which had recognised Islam, Christianity, and traditional religions although 'none of them was permitted to compromise, through constitutional and legal means, the political and civil rights of any citizens'[22]. Nimeiry's scrapping of the agreement almost immediately broke the 'peace' giving rise to the Sudan People's Liberation Movement and the Sudan People's Liberation Army (SPLM/SPLA) under John Garang.

It is significant that SPLM's programme basically sets out its goal as to build a New Sudan based on New Democracy embracing essentially all the important elements of the 'right of people to self-determination'[23]. A leading member of the organisation puts it thus:

> To bring about such a New Sudan, the edifice of the old Sudan must be destroyed in its entirety. ... The formation of the New Sudan involves two processes which must go on concurrently because of the nature of Sudan's weary historical epoch; and to be meaningful revolutions, they

> must consummate in the democracy that brings peace and prosperity to the masses of our people. The two processes are: Nation-formation and National Liberation. Nation-formation is to fuse the many nationalities in the Sudan into a nation. ...
>
> National liberation, the second process, is necessarily to liberate the Sudan from external dependency and internal exploitation[24].

But it is not only the Sudanese state, supported by Western imperialism, which has failed to implement the 'right to self-determination' but even the so-called 'socialist' state of Mengistu supported by the so-called 'developed socialist' state, the Soviet Union, has resorted to military suppression of the struggle of nations and nationalities in Ethiopia for self-determination. To be sure, even during Lenin's time, the Soviet state had begun to deviate from its principled stand on the question of self-determination[25].

To his credit, Lenin in his last days severely criticised the practice of Great-Russian chauvinism and warned of the dangers of trampling on nationality rights. That critique and warning are as valid today.

> It would be unpardonable opportunism if, on the eve of the debut of the East, just as it is awakening, we undermined our prestige with its peoples, even if only by the slightest crudity or injustice towards our own non-Russian nationalities. The need to rally against the imperialists of the West, who are defending the capitalist world, is one thing. There can be no doubt about that and it would be superfluous for me to speak about my unconditional approval of it. It is another thing when we ourselves lapse, even if only in trifles, into imperialist attitudes towards oppressed nationalities, thus undermining all our principled sincerity, all our principled defence of the struggle against imperialism[26].

The aforementioned discussion helps us to sum up one plank of the principle of political self-determination. Principally it involves the right to independence of the colonised or non-self-governing countries and the establishment of their own separate states. Cassese refers to this as the 'external' aspect of the principle. But it also involves, as a principal element, the right of oppressed nations, within otherwise sovereign states, to self-determination which ranges from some form of autonomy up to and including secession i.e. formation of a separate state. (This is the 'internal' aspect.)

The bed-rock of this principle, as all democratic principles, is the standard of equality of all nations and peoples[27]. Other elements, which are often an expression of this principle, are derivative. These are, for example, the principle of state sovereignty, territorial integrity and non-intervention. Such practices as voluntary federations and unions of nations and countries are also practices which express the principle of self-determination — the converse of secession. It is submitted that the existing state practice in Africa (including the Soviet and East European state practice) has isolated only one element in the principle, the element of anti-colonialism, and absolutised it. It has also raised the derivative element, state sovereignty and territorial integrity as well as non-intervention, to the level of the main principle and often made it the overriding element[28].

As should become clear in the course of this discussion, this practice has therefore robbed the right of self-determination of its fundamental defining characteristic — anti-imperialism. This is so because national oppression, which in Africa is often an expression of unequal and uneven national (regional) development, is derived from colonial history and perpetuated by independent states in alliance with imperialism whose local manifestation is the neo-colonial political economy.

Within the conception of national oppression and the concomitant rights are included the cultural, social and religious rights of nationalities, minorities and national groups[29]. This is recognised by the International Covenants where it is clearly stipulated that the right of peoples to self-determination includes their right to 'freely pursue their economic, social, and cultural development'[30]. Both practically and politically the full recognition and realisation of this right is extremely crucial to the democratisation process in Africa. Colonial heritage where the African people, more than any other colonised people, literally suffered cultural annihilation and oppression has not only survived but even found newer manifestations in the post-independence Africa. One of the common colonialist policies was to raise a particular nationality to the status of a favoured group in terms of education and other 'privileges' thus leaving behind not only economic but also cultural and social uneven development.

The practice of African states in this regard too has been anything but democratic as many examples from Algeria to Zimbabwe testify. The principle of non-discrimination and equality, central to the right to self-determination, is thrown overboard as some cultures, languages or religions are accorded superior status, while others are deemed inferior within the same state boundaries leading to friction and even wars. The results have been awesome as nationalities and minorities find their culture, traditions and languages despised upon and attempts made to eradicate them. This question in its own right calls for debate and discussion of practical political approaches within the larger question of democracy and anti-imperialism.

The second plank of a 'internal' aspect of political self-determination refers to the freedom of the 'people' to choose the form of their governance and government. This is where the Western doctrine and particularly propaganda relate the principle of self-determination to fundamental freedoms and human rights. But in practice Western powers themselves fall far short of implementing the anti-authoritarian thrust of this aspect of the principle. The first instrument, according to Cassese, which fully stipulates this plank in the 'internal' aspect of the principle is the Helsinki Accords where it is provided that:

> By virtue of the principle of equal rights and self-determination of peoples, all peoples always have the right, in full freedom, to determine when and as they wish, their internal and external political status, without external interference, and to pursue as they wish their political, economic, social and cultural development.

Cassese has interpreted this to mean that all peoples always have a right to choose a new social or political regime free from oppression of an authoritarian government[31]. Although somewhat weakly formulated, the African Charter could be interpreted in a similar fashion when it provides in Article 20(1):

> All peoples shall have the right to existence. They shall have the unquestionable and inalienable right to self-determination. They shall freely determine their political status and shall pursue their economic and social development according to the policy they have freely chosen.

While these formulations are capable of democratic interpretations, it does not mean that conceptions of democracy from the standpoint of the state, as opposed to that of the 'people', are necessarily the same. Indeed often they are not; for even authoritarian, compradorial states may and do go through the motions of periodic elections and setting up of representative institutions.

At this stage, what I am trying to establish is simply that the 'right to self-determination' has within it this broad democratic conceptualisation recognising fully that there are underlying tensions expressing contradictory class perspectives. I will return to this issue in my subsequent discussion on the right to organise.

The other aspect of the 'right to self-determination' is economic self-determination. Historically, the genesis of this aspect lies again in the Bolshevik Revolution of 1917. Hitherto what had reigned and exercised hegemony both in international law and practice was the right to private property. It was the Soviet state which for the first time in any significant way breached this hegemony by nationalising private property. In 1917, this was only a breach. Students of international law are familiar with the resultant contradiction in international law since then about the legitimacy or otherwise of the right to nationalise without compensation. This need not delay us further.

With the march of socialist revolutions and the upsurge of national liberation movements in the Third World, the hegemony of the right to private property was gradually but definitely eroded. While the Universal Declaration of Human Rights in 1948 still paid homage to this right, the 1966 Covenants do not include the right to private property[32]. The UN Resolution on Permanent Sovereignty over Natural Resources, 1962[33] is a further manifestation of the continuing fall in the fortunes of the sanctity of private property. However, while these developments have no doubt made serious ideological incursions into the right of private property, in practice these have been at the level of phenomenon rather than in essence. Let us explain.

Anyone familiar with Marxist and Leninist paradigms knows that the concept of private property refers to and embraces essentially the relations of exploitation between classes. Further that it is not simply confined to legal ownership of the means of production. Juridicial ownership is only one form that private property, understood as a relation of exploitation, takes under capitalism. Over a period of time, the Soviet state theory and ideology have fundamentally departed from this conceptual framework. What is counterpoised to private property is state property not social property. In other words the concept of private property is reduced to and collapsed with legal ownership of the means of production.

It is in this restricted and distorted form that the concept of private property/state property has found its way in much of the debate so far as the right to or freedom of private property is concerned.

On a more specific level, the Afro-Asian state practice has interpreted the principle of economic self-determination almost exclusively in terms of their 'trade union' demands for the so-called New International Economic Order and against some of the grossly inequitable practices of multi-national corporations, other economic institutions (e.g. World Bank, IMF etc) and the world capitalist market. These demands, which are made under the rubric of economic self-determination (the term often used is economic independence), *a fortiori* are seen as the rights of states rather than 'people'.

This conception too results in a truncated form of anti-imperialism rather than a comprehensive conceptualisation where imperialism is seen as manifesting itself in dominant/exploitative relations of production and exploitation on the economic level while socially and politically maintained by compradorial alliances which find concrete expression in authoritarian, undemocratic states.

Finally, it should be clear from the thrust of our discussion of the right that the right to self-determination is a collective right. It is a continuing right, 'a right that keeps its validity even after a people has chosen a certain form of government or a certain international status'[34]. The right-holders in the right to self-determination are dominated/exploited people and oppressed nations, nationalities, national groups and minorities identifiable specifically in each concrete situation. The duty-bearers are states, oppressor nations and nationalities and imperialist countries.

To sum up then, in the light of the foregoing discussion, the constituent elements of the 'right of people to self-determination' are:

Principal elements:
(a) equality of all peoples and nations;
(b) right of colonised people to independence and formation of their own sovereign states;
(c) right of oppressed nations to self-determination up to and including the right to secession;
(d) right of all peoples, nations, nationalities, national groups and minorities to freely pursue and develop their culture, traditions, religion and language;
(e) freedom of all peoples from alien subjugation, domination and exploitation;
(f) right of all peoples to determine democratically their own socio-economic and political system of governance and government;

Secondary or derivative elements:
(a) right of all peoples to seek assistance from other peoples in its struggle for self-determination;
(b) principle of state sovereignty, territorial integrity and non-intervention by one state in the internal affairs of another state[35].

In short, what is being proposed here is a broadening and deepening of the concept of the right to self-determination embodying the principal contradiction between imperialism and its compradorial allies vis-a-vis the people on the one hand, and oppressor vis-a-vis oppressed nations, on the other. This conceptualisation, ideologically and legally, captures the most important elements of the anti-imperialist democratic struggles within the framework of a New Democratic Revolution as at the same time showing historical continuity with democracy in general and revolutionary tradition in particular. During its revolutionary days the Chinese Communist Party summed up the main trends in the Third World as:

Countries want Independence;
Nations want Liberation and
People want revolution.

The reconceptualisation of the 'right to self-determination' attempts to capture these trends on an ideological/legal plane within the framework of human rights discourse.

It is further submitted that conceptualised as it is here, the 'right to self-determination' is superior to and has advantages over the so-called 'right to development'. This is discussed next.

Right to self-determination and right to development compared

The genesis of the right to self-determination lies in the struggles of the people from the days of bourgeois revolutions in the 18th-19th century Europe to the post-war national liberation struggles of the people of the Third World. It thus has historical legitimacy which the right to development does not. The right to development finds its roots in the contemporary demands of the Third World states for better terms on the international market, greater aid and assistance and generally in, what has come to be known as, the demand for the new international economic order.

At best these are statist 'trade union' demands which seek a little more comfortable accommodation for the Third World ruling classes within the existing order. At worst, they amount to no more than a new way of asserting a 'right' to charity.

On the level of international law, as the right to self-determination has developed over more than half a century, it has come to be recognised by international law and has found place in UN treaties (the 1966 Covenants) as well as in a considerable number of other international treaties among states of both the North and the South[36]. To be sure, the conceptualisation and the content of this right, as we have seen, remains contentious as indeed it should, given the underlying contradictions of the world imperialist system. That it captures some of these important contradictions is its strength rather than weakness.

The right to development, on the other hand, is an assertion of a 'new' right. It does not therefore have the legitimacy of international legality. True, its development has been fast from the original conception to the Declaration by the General Assembly. It has been enthusiastically taken over by liberals of the West, supported by Soviet-oriented theorists and almost unanimously advocated by African international lawyers. Even if it eventually finds a place in an international covenant, the question remains: Does it serve the interests of the people of Africa?

Conceptually the right to development has very weak foundations. Development itself has either been expanded to include everything (and therefore nothing!) as in the UN Declaration[37], or more often narrowed to economic development in its economistic, and increasingly, even econometric sense. Either way it blunts, if not eliminates, the ideological and political sting and sharpness which are central to the concept of self-determination.

Under the right of self-determination, the right-holders are a collective whether people, nations, nationalities or national groups. Besides the fact that each one of these concepts has strong theoretical foundations, they are practically and politically of immediate relevance to Africa in its struggle against imperialism and authoritarianism.

Secondly, these concepts are not tied to existing state structures and system but rather have an independent dynamism of their own with a capacity to comprehend and guide change. In a word, they express class struggle rather than a statist status quo. The concept of the right to development, on the contrary, is both static as well as statist. The right here generally belongs to 'states' as is clearly expressed in the Declaration. The Preamble 'recognises' that 'the creation of conditions favourable to the development of peoples and individuals is the primary responsibility of their States'. 'States have the right and duty to formulate appropriate national development policies', (art.2(3)); States have a duty to co-operate with each other in ensuring development (art.3(3)) and in formulating international development policies (art.4(1)); even popular participation is supposed to be encouraged by states (art.8(2)) and 'States should fulfil their rights and duties in such a manner as to promote a new international economic order based on sovereign equality, interdependence, mutual interest and co-operation among all States, as well as to encourage the observance and realization of human rights', (art.3(3)).

The 'State' here has been presented out from a fairy-tale as the embodiment of all virtues and interests of the people which, needless to say, flies in the face of historical evidence and is certainly nowhere close to the real-life authoritarian states of Africa used ruthlessly by imperialism and compradorial ruling classes in the exploitation and oppression of the African people and nations.

Finally, underlying the right to development is a conception which sees development/democracy as a gift/charity from above rather than the result of struggles from below. On the international plane, it is based on an illusory model of co-operation and solidarity (*a là* M'Baye). This is like crying for the moon, for how can there be solidarity between a rider and the horse?

Under the right to development the human person is seen as a 'participant and beneficiary' (art.2(1)) of development where, development therefore, is someone else's (state's?!) project. Under self-determination people are themselves the creators of, and the struggling force for, development and democracy which are reclaimed and asserted as their project. People are neither pitiable victims of state's excesses nor recipients of state's handouts. In the latter conceptualisation, the state takes its rightful place as a historical and social category both as a participant in and an embodiment of class struggles.

The right to development fits in neatly in the ideology of developmentalism which has been the hallmark of African states since independence in rationalising the depoliticisation and demobilisation of the African masses. It has managed to occupy many conferences and discussions. Given its spurious nature, in our opinion it has played a diversionary role in shifting attention from the reality of the Third World and its struggling people.

Right to Organise

If the right to self-determination expresses the principal contradiction between imperialism and the people on the international plane with significant implications on the national/municipal level, the right to organise expresses the principal contradiction between the exploited working people and the compradorial state on the national/municipal level with significant implications on the international plane. We are arguing for the centrality of these rights on the respective levels. The two are inseparable and indivisible and really two sides of the same coin at this stage of the African revolution.

Elsewhere, I have argued that the ruling ideology in the post-independence Africa may be characterised as the ideology of developmentalism. This ideology is very simple. It takes its point of departure the real material conditions, the conditions of underdevelopment, and argues that therefore development takes priority over everything else. It is said Africa can ill-afford the luxury of politics. Therefore in this ideological paradigm, politics is displaced while economics prevails on the ideological terrain. The fact that politics is banished from the ideological discourse does not mean that it disappears from real life. As a matter of fact, in practice, as can now be verified from the experience of the last three decades, it is the politics of the people that is displaced while the politics of the ruling class is consolidated. Depoliticisation of the masses constitutes the politics of the ruling classes.

The ideology of developmentalism, therefore, serves as a

rationalisation of the politics of the ruling class under which the state and the ruling class establish their organisational hegemony over the people through the demobilisation of the masses. This is accompanied by a two-fold trend. On the level of the state, power is concentrated in the executive/military arms as the various representative organs such as Parliament etc., are marginalised or drained of their democratic content. On the level of civil society, various mass organisations are suppressed and usurped by the state thus mutilating, if not destroying, the organisational capacity of the people.

The result is an authoritarian state, which in Africa today, is a typical expression of the rule of compradorial classes in alliance with imperialism. This state may take various forms, from military dictatorships to the so-called one-party democracies. The consequence of these developments has been that the people have lost out both on development as well as democracy. No wonder that they are least equipped to resist encroachment on their rights.

In the present conjuncture of the democratic struggle, therefore, the demand/struggle for the right to organise becomes very significant as the people have to reclaim their organisational initiative and rebuild their organisational capacity independent from and without interference of the state. (And here we are referring to all kinds of civil organisations from peasant associations, through trade unions to political parties).

Traditionally, the right to organise, often expressed as right to or freedom of association, except in the ILO Conventions, is conceptualised as an individual right of every person to associate with a fellow person, on the basis of certain common interests. Although there is nothing in the formulation to support such an interpretation, this right has come to be associated with organisations of civil/economic nature rather than political/ideological. The latter, more specifically political parties, are subsumed within the discussion of democratic/political system rather than a right *per se*.

The International Commission of Jurists, in its famous Dar-es-Salaam seminar in 1976, even reached the conclusion that democratic government is possible within a one-party system and that this need not necessarily impair the right of association. Here a clear distinction is drawn between civil and political organisation while the right to organise is restricted to the former.

The formulation of this right in various documents, ranging from municipal constitutions to international UN-sponsored conventions and regional instruments, has varied from a fairly broad to a very narrow and restrictive definition. Thus the Universal Declaration is scanty on this. It simply provides, 'Everyone has the right to freedom of peaceful assembly and association', (art.20). The 1966 Covenants, on the other hand, are a little more elaborate and specifically refer to the right to form and join trade unions, (art.8 of the Social and Cultural and art.22 of the Civil and Political Covenants).

It could be argued with some justification, that the right to form political parties is not envisaged within these provisions. The ILO Convention on the *Freedom of Association and Protection of the Right to Organise* (1948) is probably the most comprehensive and the most protective formulation with regard to trade unions.

> Article 2
>
> Workers and employers, without distinction whatsoever, shall have the right to establish and, subject only to the rules of the organisation concerned, to join organisations of their own choosing without previous authorization.
>
> Article 3
>
> 1. Workers' and employers' organisations shall have the right to draw up their constitutions and rules, to elect their representatives in full freedom, to organise their administration and activities and to formulate their programmes.
> 2. The public authorities shall refrain from any interference which would restrict this right or impede the lawful exercise thereof.
>
> Article 4
>
> Workers' and employers' organisations shall not be liable to be dissolved or suspended by administrative authority.
>
> Article 8
>
> 2. The law of the land shall not be such as to impair, nor shall it be so applied as to impair, the guarantees provided for in this Convention.

These standards in the case of trade unions are hardly met in any of the African countries[38]. It is significant that while both the European and American Conventions specifically provide for the freedom to form and join trade unions, the African Charter does not. And its formulation of the freedom of association is probably also the weakest[39].

Furthermore, while the most common derogation permissible is usually only in circumstances 'prescribed by law and necessary in a democratic society in the interests of national security or public order or for the protection of the rights and freedoms of others'[40], the African Charter gives a blank cheque for restrictions as the individual's right to free association is subject to his abiding by the law,(art.10(1)).

All in all, it should not be surprising that African states are wary of this right. Their opposition to the right to organise is an important expression of state authoritarianism.

Like the right to self-determination, the right to organise has also to be conceptually broadened and deepened to cover the most important interests of the working people at this stage. Firstly, we submit that this right should be seen as a collective and not an individual right. The notion of an autonomous individual associating with other autonomous individuals is typically Hobbesian and, as I have argued, has no historical or social validity much less relevance to the contemporary African situation.

Secondly, the dichotomy between civil and political organisations is also irrelevant and as a matter of fact not in the ideological interests of the African people. This dichotomy falls squarely within the ideology of developmentalism and shares its assumptions as well as social character. Conceptually, it is suggested, the right to organise is a fundamental right of the people to come together on various levels for the protection of their interests and for resistance to oppression and domination.

As with the right to self-determination, so with the right to organise: it extends up to and includes the right to make a revolution where the people find that their interests are not served by a particular social, economic and political order. As a matter of fact, this is no great departure from the historical antecedents of the human rights idea. The famous American Declaration of the Rights of Man of 1776, while proclaiming self-evident truths and inalienable rights, in the same breath declared 'That whenever any Form of Government becomes destructive of these ends (these rights -I.G.), it is the Right of the People to alter or to abolish it, and to institute a new Government, ...'[41]. The French Declaration of 1789 included among its 'sacred' rights the right to 'resistance of oppression'. It said:

> The end of all political associations is the preservation of the natural and imprescriptible rights of man; and these rights are liberty, property, security, and resistance of oppression.

As one commentator has observed 'Early declarations of rights were regarded as justifications for revolution...'[42].

To sum up, the most important elements of the right to organise are:

(a) It is an inalienable collective right of the people and social groups to organise freely for ideological, religious, political, economic, labour, social, cultural, sports, or other purposes[43].

(b) Its exercise shall not be interfered with in any way or form by the state or any other public authority save on grounds of immediate danger to public health or morality.

(c) It shall not be derogable except in circumstances provided for by law and necessary in a democratic society in cases of present and imminent danger to the nation and its independence or on grounds of public health.

(d) The right to organise includes and extends to the right to resist oppression, authoritarianism and any other undemocratic practices.

In short then, the right to organise is a central democratic right and crucial at the present stage in Africa to reinvigorate the capacity of the people to self-organise in their long struggle for social emancipation. We see autonomous (independent of the state-party) organisations of the people as so many schools of democracy which, it is submitted, are necessary in the march towards building New Democratic states in Africa: nationally independent and liberated; socially rooted in the working people and politically democratic.

HUMAN RIGHTS ACTIVITY

As we have seen, there is a dearth of human rights NGOs in Africa. And that is typical of the entire organisational scene insofar as autonomous organisations of civil society are concerned. Yet the importance of people's autonomous organisations cannot be gainsaid. The broad masses have to regain and rebuild their organisational capacity mutilated by the compradorial neo-colonial states. Thus NGOs, human rights and others, have an added significance and a greater political role in Africa compared to the developed capitalist countries where they are taken for granted.

Our critique of the mainstream positions, however, means that the local human rights NGOs (LONGOS) must be characterised by certain shifts and biases. Firstly, they have to clearly distance themselves from imperialist funded organisations. Hitherto, as was observed earlier, very often these organisations have tended to degenerate into simple mechanisms for obtaining foreign funds. As a matter of fact, even African governments have begun to encourage formation of local NGOs (which they control — GONGOs) with an eye on getting funds as Western governments are inclined to funnel their funds more and more through NGOs rather than government bureaucracies. Genuine people's NGOs cannot either be FFUNGOs (foreign funded NGOs) or GONGOs (government organised NGOs) if they are to serve the purpose that we have been outlining in this work.

Secondly, these organisations have to distance themselves from the authoritarian state structures. It is again a tendency of elite-led NGOs in Africa to put themselves at the service of the state. They go out of their way to offer their services to authoritarian states. Clearly, such organisations compromise themselves strategically and are thus disabled from serving the interests of the people.

Thirdly, such organisations will have to move away from elitist orientations if they are to do genuine grass-root work among the people. Protection and promotion of human rights is not some 'expert' business to be carried out by the so-called intellectuals on behalf of the masses. Only the people themselves can protect and fight for their rights. Intellectuals and other activists can only join in that struggle.

Given these 'guidelines' one can probably broadly discuss some kinds of LONGO human rights activity which would be relevant while being at the same time within the new conceptualisation suggested in this work. To be sure, the details and concrete forms emerge and will emerge from the actual struggles of the people. First and foremost, therefore, it is these struggles that have to be turned into a source of both new forms of organisations as well as new forms of struggle for human rights.

As for some of the known forms of human rights organisations and activity, in spite of political constraints, experience shows that there are possibilities which have not always been utilised to the fullest. Law and legal aid related activity is one of these. African Bar associations and lawyers' organisations *per se* have generally proved to be pretty conservative and reactionary, but university-based legal aid schemes hold out greater prospect for human rights activity.

In this respect, two further avenues of development have to be explored. One, legal aid activity has to develop in the direction of legal aid movement with the participation of the broad sections of the community in perhaps neighbourhood groups. The Indonesian[44] and Phillipine experiences, in this respect, are worth learning from. The other direction of development is the broadening and deepening of what has come to be known in India as public-interest or social-action litigation[45]. This involves class-action litigation, not necessarily by the injured parties themselves, but by public interest groups. To our knowledge, these developments have not in any way influenced legal aid activity in Africa.

The other forum most often neglected is the church and other religious-based organisations. While these do pose political problems, yet they offer an arena of human rights activity which may not yet have been used to the fullest.

Trade unions, women's, students, and youth organisations too can play a very important role in human rights struggles. These too have often been neglected by African human rights activists.

Professional and academic organisations in Africa tend to occupy themselves with elitist concerns. Yet they can make some crucial contribution, particularly in highlighting and exposing human rights issues. The commitment made by some 140 prominent Arab intellectuals some two years ago is worthy of emulation. This is what their statement said:

> ...Many of our daily activities stand in absolute contradiction with what we call for. This inconsistency is manifest in the explicit or implicit collaboration with repressive regimes. What appears to be beyond the control of the intellectual within his/her country does not force him/her to collaborate with regimes in other countries with the same record of violation of human rights. For, at least, that which cannot be wholly achieved, should not be entirely renounced.
>
> Bearing this in mind we call upon all Arab intellectuals who believe in the respect of human rights to abstain from taking part in any cultural or political activity organized or financed by any Arab regime which violates the basic human rights of the Arab individual. This should apply, among other things, to the participation in congresses and seminars, to the collaboration with 'research centres', to writing in journals and magazines and all other practices which represent part of the external propaganda of this regime and in which the participation of the intellectual might contribute, one way or the other, to giving a sort of legitimacy to this regime[46].

Then there are pan-African organisations. It seems to me these organisations can be effective only if they have branches and chapters effectively doing grass-root human rights work. On the continental level such an organization cannot gain any credibility if it panders to the wishes of the African states. Rather, it should be seriously involved in exposing situations which are responsible for human rights violations.

Ultimately, it seems to me, human rights activity cannot be separated from the general struggle of the people against oppression. In other words, human rights struggles are an integral part of general social movements and that is where human rights activity should be presently located.

NOTES

1. V. I. Lenin, *A Caricature of Marxism and Imperialist Economism* (Moscow: Progress Publishers, 1974), p.22 (emphasis in the original).
2. The fact that in some cases even the Soviet Union has supported undemocratic regimes in no way refutes our argument. Apart from its consistent support for anti-colonial struggles, Soviet revisionism has exhibited strong 'imperialist' tendencies in its relations with post-colonial African countries.
3. This is in no way to refute a truism that in social struggles, a new type of struggle is often expressed through the 'old' cultural images even though it may have a progressive political and social content. What is being critiqued here is a reactionary approach to traditions and culture where they are used in their atrophied forms to serve the ideological purposes of the ruling classes in the interest of maintaining the *status quo*. Similarly, no anti-imperialist, democratic struggle can dismiss the question of development *per se*. But as I have repeatedly argued, the ideology of developmentalism has little to do with genuine national development; rather it is an attempt to legitimise the rule of the compradorial classes and continued imperialist domination and exploitation of the working people.
4. I am thinking of such concepts as the 'state of the whole people', 'socialist-oriented states', 'political parties of the masses led by revolutionary democrats', 'developed socialism' (as opposed to what?!) etc. so much in vogue in the Soviet literature.
5. See V. I. Lenin, *Selected Works*, vol. 2, p. 475.
6. Akram H. Chowdhury, 'The Question of Self-determination of Indigenous Populations under International Law: The Case of Chittagong Hill Tracts', mimeo. CODESRIA Documents, pp.7 et.seq.
7. Antonio Cassese, 'Political Self-determination — Old Concepts and New Developments', in Cassese (ed.), *op.cit.*, p.138.
8. It was included in the UN Declaration on the Granting of Independence to Colonial Countries adopted on 14 December 1960 when significantly USA, Great Britain, France, Belgium, Portugal, South Africa, Australia, Dominican Republic and Spain abstained. *Ibid.*, p.141.
9. Ian Brownlie, *Principles of Public International Law* (Oxford: Clarendon Press,1979) 3rd.edn.,p.593.
10. See *Selected Works*, vol. 1, *op.cit.*, pp.598-9.
11. Lenin, 'The Discussion on Self-determination Summed Up', in Lenin, *On the National Question and Proletarian Internationalism* (Moscow: Novosty Press, 1970) p.100.
12. Quoted in Tunkin (ed.), *op.cit.*, pp.46-9.
13. Cassese has argued that the formulation of this principle in the *Helsinki Accords* goes further than the traditional UN and Soviet position on self-determination. The Soviet Union itself had suggested the 'traditional' formulation. But the fact that it finally agreed to the broader formulation shows the Soviet Union's pragmatic rather than principled position on this issue and even discriminatory approaches depending on whether it is dealing with weaker Afro-Asian countries or fellow super-powers in Europe, Cassese, *op.cit.*, pp.148-53. For the text of the Helsinki Accords see Brownlie, *Human Rights*, *op.cit.*, p.320.
14. See Selassie, *op.cit.*
15. Op.cit, *p.140.*
16. See Mamdani, *op.cit.*
17. Witness the refugee situation in Africa. With one-tenth of the world population, Africa is estimated to have almost half the world's refugees. And the majority

of these refugees have run away from political oppression and problems of civil wars in their countries. See Kannyo, 'Banjul Charter', in Welch & Meltzer, *op.cit.*, p.131, p.137. See also Zdenek Cervenka, 'The effects of militarisation of Africa on Human Rights', *Africa To-day,* vol.34:69-84 (1987).

18. Lam Akol, 'The Present War and Its Solution', in Francis Mading Deng and Prosser Gifford (eds.), *The Search for Peace and Unity in the Sudan* (Washington: The Wilson Center Press, 1987), pp.15-23 at p.15.
19. Mohammed Beshir Hamid, 'Devolution and the Problems of National Integration in the Sudan', *Ethnic Studies Report II, no.2,* July 1984, p.61. See also SPLM/SPLA publication *Sudan Today*, (London: 1985).
20. B. Yongo-Bure, 'Prospects for Socio-economic Development of the South', in Deng & Prosser (eds.) *op.cit.*, pp.36-50 at p.48.
21 Elias Nyamlell Wakoson, 'The Dilemmas of South-North Conflict', in Deng & Prosser (eds.) *op.cit.*, pp.90-106 at p.92 and Mansour Khalid,'External Factors in the Sudanese Conflict', in *ibid.*, pp.109-26 at p.113.
22. Bona Malwal, 'The Roots of Current Contention', in *ibid.*, pp.7-14 at p.14.
23. See Akol, *op.cit.*, p.16 *et seq.*
24. *Ibid.*, p.20.
25. See Lenin, 'The Question of Nationalities or Autonomisation', in Lenin, *On the National Question*, *op.cit.* pp.141 *et seq.*
26. *Ibid.*, p.148.
27. On the concept of equality in International Law see the Dissenting Opinion of Judge Tanaka in the 'South West Africa Cases (Second Phase), 1966' reproduced in Brownlie, *Human Rights*, *op.cit.*, pp. 441-70.
28. See for instance the OAU Charter and Cassese, *Op. cit.*
29. The use of these concepts is not without problems. In the bourgeois 'international law' jurisprudence, as a matter of fact, these concepts are used most confusedly where often state, country, nation, people etc. are used interchangeably. In the Marxist literature, on the other hand, these terms have a definite conceptual content. The use of these terms in this work is in the latter tradition. However, it must be pointed out that 'minority' is not part of the Marxist conceptual framework and does pose some theoretical problems. For an example of total confusion on these concepts in the bourgeois literature see Yoram Dinstein, 'Collective Human Rights of Peoples and Minorities', in *International Comparative and Law Quarterly* 25:102-20 (1976) where the meaning of the terms 'nation' and 'people' is reversed. This confusion. however, may not be totally innocent; it is probably meant to justify the claims of zionists to a separate state.
30. Vernon Van Dyke, 'The Cultural Rights of Peoples', *Universal Human Rights* 2, no.2:1-21 (April-June, 1980).
31. *Op.cit.*, p.152.
32. Interestingly even the European Convention seems to give it an inferior status by including it in the First Protocol, more or less as an afterthought.
33. Resolution 1803 (XVII).
34. Cassese, *op.cit.*, p.150.
35. Notice that here the concept of 'people' is primary and state is seen as subordinate, rather than the other way round as in the existing literature.
36. The Helsinki Accords and the OAU Charter, for example.
37. The Preamble states: ...

    That development is a comprehensive economic, social, cultural and political process, which aims at the constant improvement of the well-being of the entire population and of all individuals on the basis of their active, free and meaningful participation in development and in the fair distribution of benefits resulting therefrom,

38. Rhoda, *Human Rights, op.cit.*, pp.128-33. For trade unions in Tanzania see Shivji, *Law, State and the Working Class op.cit.*, ch.7; for comparison with Ghana see Claude E. Welch, 'The Right of Association in Ghana and Tanzania', *Journal of Modern African Studies* 16, no.4:639-56 (1978). For the suppression of trade unionists in Tunisia see AI, USA: Tunisia: *Trade Unionists Jailed* (April,1979). For the right of association in Nigeria and Sudan see Akinola Aguda & Oluwadere Aguda, 'Judicial Protection of Some Fundamental Rights in Nigeria and the Sudan before and during Military Rule', *Journal of African Law* 16, no.2:130-44 (1972), at pp.139-40. Just at the beginning of 1988 the Babangida government moved against the Nigerian Trade Union Congress by sacking its leadership on the typical excuse that they were spending more time on ideological disputes rather than serving the interests of workers. It went ahead and appointed a General Manager of a large private company to look after the assets of the Congress! (BBC Focus on Africa Report, 1 March 1988).
39. Steven Neff, *Human Rights in Botswana, Lesotho and Swaziland: Implications of adherence to International Human Rights Treaties* (Lesotho: Institute of Southern African Studies, 1986), p.8.
40. This formulation is to be found in the International Covenant on Social and Economic Rights, art.8.
41. Quoted in Eugene Kamenka, 'The anatomy of an idea', in Kamenka & Tay (eds.), *op.cit.*, p.2.
42. Kleinig, *op.cit.*, p.44.
43. This formulation is taken from the American Convention, art.16(1).
44. See Buyung Nasution, 'The Legal Aid Movement in Indonesia: Towards the Implementation of the Structural Legal Aid Concept', in Scoble & Wiseberg, *Access to Justice op.cit.*, pp.31-9. For limitations of legal aid work see T. Mulya Lubis, 'Legal Aid: Some Reflections', in ibid., pp.40-3 and Issa G. Shivji, 'Within and Beyond Legal Radicalism', in Issa G. Shivji, *Limits of Legal Radicalism: Reflections on Teaching Law at the University of Dar-es-Salaam* (Dar-es-Salaam: Faculty of Law, 1986), pp.117-33.
45. Upendra Baxi, 'Taking Suffering Seriously: Social Action Litigation in the Supreme Court of India', in the ICJ Review no. 29:37-9 (December, 1982) and sources cited therein.
46. 'Arab Intellectuals Stand in Defense of Human Rights', in IFDA *Dossier*, no.53:69-70 (May/June, 1986).

4. DOMINANT AND REVOLUTIONARY TENDENCIES ILLUSTRATED

INTRODUCTION

Broadly the two tendencies in human rights, which may be characterised as 'dominant' and 'revolutionary', are manifested respectively in a concrete form in the African Charter on Human and People's Rights adopted by the eighteenth OAU Summit Meeting held in Nairobi in June 1981 and the Universal Declaration of the Rights of Peoples (known as the Algiers Declaration, see the Appendix) adopted by a group of 'jurists, political scientists, sociologists, representatives of trade unions and political parties of various countries, as well as members of several liberation movements'[1] at a meeting held in Algiers on 4 July 1976. These documents express on various levels what may be considered the quintessence of the two tendencies. The primary aim in this chapter is to demonstrate how the African Charter tendentially represents the philosophical/ideological outlook, the political/practical approach and the social standpoint implied by and inherent in the dominant discourse. The Algiers Declaration, on the other hand, crystallizes the alternative conception advocated in this work. Within their own paradigms, these documents no doubt have some severe limitations and the African Charter particularly has been widely criticised. Nonetheless, these criticisms, some of which will be highlighted in the course of the discussion, are internal to and within the major premises of the diametrically opposed conceptions.

HISTORICAL ANTECEDENTS

Observers have emphasised a number of external and internal factors which went into precipitating the decision by the OAU to commission a Human Rights Charter at its meeting in Monrovia in 1979. Carter came to power in the US in 1977 'committed' to an active human rights policy in conducting his foreign affairs.[2] As has been conclusively shown by researchers of various shades, this was no more than a rhetoric meant for internal consumption[3]. Coupled with emphasis on 'violations' of human rights in the Soviet Union, Carter's human rights activism was meant to salvage the US morally and reestablish the state's legitimacy after the Vietnam debacle and the Watergate scandal and drum up cold-war hysteria in a new form.

While the Carter administration continued to support and arm fascist dictators (Shah of Iran; Mobutu of Zaire; Hassan of Morocco; Suharto of Indonesia; Botha of South Africa, to mention but a few) in the main, it had inevitably to produce a few peripheral actions, such as linking of 'aid' to human rights record, to show its seriousness. Given their dependence on imperialist handouts, African states had to fall in line and produce in turn their own rhetoric to reestablish their 'aid-worthiness'[4].

The rise and fall of the three most brutal dictators (Amin of Uganda, 1971-79; Nguema of Equatorial Guinea, 1968-79 and Bokassa of the Central African Empire, 1966-1979)[5] during the decade of the seventies had severely tarnished the human rights image of Africa. Like Carter, African Presidents in the OAU had to salvage their own credibility. (With one important difference: whereas Carter's human rights rhetoric was primarily for domestic consumption, OAU's was largely for international, particularly Western consumption!) But even more significant, and probably the immediate cause that precipitated the Monrovia decision, was the invasion of Uganda by the Tanzanian forces resulting in Amin's overthrow. Earlier Nyerere had insisted that the OAU condemn Idi Amin rather than continue with its long-established tradition of the 'trade union of the current Heads of State and Government, with solidarity reflected in silence if not in open support for each other'[6] even when one of them was involved in organised brutality against his own people. That outburst went unheeded as some twenty Heads of State and Government met in Kampala for an OAU Summit in 1975 and proclaimed Idi Amin as its Chairman. Later, when the Tanzanian forces invaded Uganda and overthrew Amin, that action drew severe criticisms from some OAU members. The 1979 Monrovia Summit censored Nyerere with Nimeiry, Tolbert and Obasanjo leading the attack accusing the President of Tanzania of setting a bad precedent, interfering in the internal affairs of a member state and violating the principle of territorial integrity[7]. Nonetheless, the Monrovia Summit by then was shaken enough to appoint a committee of experts to prepare a draft of an 'African Charter of Human and People's Rights'. The Charter, as we shall see, bears the birthmarks of essentially a neo-colonialist, statist disposition and concerns of its founding fathers.

The Algiers Declaration rests on a different foundation. It arose in the context of a Third World in upsurge and an international situation in turmoil. The US defeat in Vietnam, the Kampuchean revolution, the victory of the national liberation movements in Mozambique, Angola and Guinea-Bissau immensely raised the prestige of, and a hope for, people's movements in Africa and Asia. In that context, progressive intellectuals, representatives of liberation movements and trade unions, in their own individual capacity, met in Algiers under the auspices of the Lelio Basso Foundation[8]. They were unencumbered by statist concerns and dominant ideological predilections which proclaim human rights issues to be apolitical and neutral. As Francois Rigaux notes:

> By dividing up its object, science — especially the science of law — has managed to render social reality aseptic. Only a larva can live in a test-tube and the very success of the so-called human or social sciences has helped to depoliticise our thinking. In this sense, the Algiers declaration is profoundly political, because its inspiration is a global reflection on the real conditions in which people are actually living[9].

IDEOLOGICAL UNDERPINNINGS AND SOCIAL CHARACTER

The Algiers Declaration is people-centred. 'The 'fathers of the Declaration wanted to look beyond the phraseology of national constitutions or the Preamble of the United Nations Charter towards the new subject of international law, the people, whose collective rights have all too often been concealed by the classic human rights approach, just as the wood is hidden by the trees'[10]. This shift from individualistic to collectivist approach is fundamental. 'By a means of a sort of Copernican revolution it moves the centre of gravity of international law from the individual and the State (this hypertrophied individual which is sometimes a Moloch or a Chronos that devours its own children) towards the peoples'[11]. The categories 'individual' and 'state' are simply absent from the Declaration where every article on rights begins 'Every people...'.

Conversely, the African Charter only raises the shadow of 'people's rights', while remaining firmly anchored in the substance of 'individual and state rights'. It is decisively state-centred, confirming the practice of the OAU and its member states since its inception[12]. Examination of its substantive provisions shows that it is primarily the 'state' which is seen as a collective representative of the people in the African Charter. There are only six articles on people's rights out of a total of 26 articles on rights. Half of these are hortatory such as right to equality (art.19), to existence (art.20), to 'national and international peace and security' (art.23) and to 'environment favourable to their development' (art.24). The other three, which relate to the more substantive subject-matter, grant rights to 'people' but in the same breath make them exercisable by the state. Article 21(1) stipulates broadly that 'All peoples shall freely dispose of their wealth and natural resources' while paragraph 3 immediately follows on the heels to curtail the freedom just granted in that the right 'shall be exercised without prejudice to the ... principles of international law'.

These principles still recognise such things as fair and reasonable compensation for any re-take-over by the people of their wealth and natural resources which in Africa are monopolised and garnered by multinationals and imperial capital[13]. And paragraph 4 wraps up in a grandiose language what really are some kind of 'trade union' (OPEC type?) aspirations of the African compradorial states who 'shall individually and collectively exercise the right to free disposal of their wealth and natural resources with a view to strengthening African unity and solidarity'. Even the struggle against multinationals is projected into the unknown future as 'States parties to the Charter shall undertake to eliminate all forms of foreign economic exploitation particularly that practised by international monopolies', (paragraph 5).[14]. The same rhetoric of people's rights and state's prerogative of exercise is evident in article 22 which proclaims that 'All peoples shall have the right to their economic, social and cultural development' while the next paragraph deceptively using the term 'duty' records the small print, 'States shall have the duty, individually and collectively, to ensure the exercise of the right to development'.

Ideologically the Algiers Declaration clearly proclaims its anti-imperialist stand thus:

> This is ... a time of frustration and defeat, as new forms of imperialism evolve to oppress and exploit the peoples of the world. Imperialism, using vicious methods, with the complicity of governments that it has itself often installed, continues to dominate a part of the world. Through direct or indirect intervention, through multinational enterprises, through manipulation of corrupt local politicians, with the assistance of military regimes based on police repression, torture and physical extermination of opponents, through a set of practices that has become known as neo-colonialism, imperialism extends its stranglehold over many peoples[15].

The Declaration does not make any pretence at being an international instrument dedicated to refining human rights standards or evolving further mechanisms of enforcement but rather puts itself forward as an ideological legitimiser and a political manifesto of peoples struggling against an oppressive status quo. In this it follows the principled historical traditions of all great declarations of rights, from Magna Carta to the Soviet Declaration of the Rights of the Working and Exploited People as opposed to the expedient diplomatic postures of international conventions. The Algiers Declaration makes a clarion call:

> May all those who, throughout the world, are fighting the great battle, at times through armed struggle, for the freedom of all peoples, find in this Declaration the assurance of the legitimacy of their struggle[16].

There are three ideological themes that run through the African Charter: anti-colonialism and anti-racism; developmentalism and the so-called international co-operation[17]. Anti-colonialism is a partial or limited form of anti-imperialism, where imperialism is conflated into formal colonialism. In this regard, therefore, what remains of 'colonialism' is South Africa and Namibia. Both the African rhetoric as well as the Charter do use such terminology as neo-colonialism, foreign exploitation etc[18]. In practice, this is meant to refer to the inequities of the international market system whose solution is seen in the so-called New International Economic Order. (This is what we have been referring to in this work as the 'trade union' conception of the world imperialist system held by the African ruling classes.)

Developmentalism is proclaimed in the Preamble, which for the first time in an international legal instrument, refers to the 'right to development'. Developmentalism domestically manifests itself in the various arguments about expediency of economic development, often used to justify non-democratic politics[19]. On the international level, it expresses itself in the demands for NIEO already referred to above.

Both the OAU Charter and the African Charter go out of their way to pay obeisance to 'international co-operation'. This is not simply a diplomatic ritual. Rather it is a significant ideological stance with a profound meaning and reflection of the dependent character of the African states and their weak bourgeois ruling classes. International co-operation has a two-fold meaning, on the African level and the international level. On the international level it expresses the dependence on imperialist 'aid' and 'investment' as has been so deftly packaged in the so-called 'right to development' which we have already critiqued. On the African level it is expressed in the principles of territorial integrity, state sovereignty and non-intervention and non-interference in internal affairs. It is a kind of mutual pact on the part of the African Heads of State and Government to leave one another as free as possible to do what they want to within their own jurisdictions[20]. Given their general weakness, the bourgeoisies in Africa can never let go the control of their states, particularly vis-a-vis other African states. This is what really lies behind the mutual mistrust among them on the one hand and the zealous guarding of their state sovereignty on the other. It is also an expression of their authoritarian character in relation to their own people which they can ill-afford to be exposed; hence non-interference in internal affairs. At the Monrovia Summit, Sekou Toure of Guinea[21] probably spoke for many African Heads of State when he asserted that the OAU was not 'a tribunal which could sit in judgment on any members state's internal affairs'[22]. Thus international co-operation on the African level means to co-operate to keep silent on each other's conduct.

Finally, one of the partial 'innovations' of the African Charter is also at the same time an ideological reflection of the authoritarian character of the African neo-colonial state. This is the concept of 'duty' of an individual. This concept is totally absent from the European Convention. The liberal tradition of individual human rights is of course predicated on placing the duty for the respect of those rights on the state. As we have seen, historically it arose from the need to restrict the powers of the absolutist states in Europe. The American Convention, 1969[23] does have a concept of duty but significantly different from the one in the African Charter. In just one article, the American Convention stipulates in very general terms a person's 'responsibilities to his family, his community, and mankind' and that 'the rights of each person are limited by the rights of others, by the security of all, and by the just demands of the general welfare, in a democratic society', (art.32)[24].

The Secretary General of the OAU particularly enjoined upon the Experts drafting the Charter to determine, among other things, 'the duties of each person towards the community in which he lives and more particularly towards the family and the state'[25]. In Chapter II, where the duties of the individual are stipulated, probably the most significant innovation peculiar to the African Charter is the specific mention of duties to the state, the most important of which are enumerated as:

> Not to compromise the security of the State whose national or resident he is;
> To preserve and strengthen social and national integrity, particularly when the latter is threatened;

> To preserve and strengthen the national independence and the territorial integrity of his country and to contribute to its defence in accordance with the law; (art.29(3-5))

Article 18(1) provides that 'the family shall be the natural basis of society. It shall be protected by the State which shall take care of its physical health and moral'. As if that were not enough, paragraph 2 obliges the state to 'assist the family which is the custodian of moral and traditional values recognised by the community'.

Read as a whole, and taking into account the notorious authoritarian practices of African states, it is clear that what is demanded of the African people in this catalogue of duties is absolute allegiance to the existing State and the institution of the family — both of which respectively represent, politically and historically, retrogression. To dramatise a bit, these provisions read like Mobutu's authenticity or Banda's traditionalism on the pan-African level and probably bearing the same rationale.

These ideological 'biases' find manifestation concretely in other provisions as well. Significantly, they are even more blatantly deficient in the formulation and stipulation of what we consider the central rights — the 'right to self-determination' and the 'right to organise'. These are examined below.

RIGHT TO SELF-DETERMINATION IN THE AFRICAN CHARTER AND THE ALGIERS DECLARATION

I have already argued that the African Charter confines the right to political self-determination ('external') to colonial, non-self-governing countries. There is, therefore, no right of oppressed nations within the sovereign states to secede. Territorial integrity is upheld at all cost. 'In effect, then, Article 20(1) gives sovereign states the right to self-determination, while Article 29 seems to deny this right to communities within sovereign states'[26]. Nor does the Charter take account of the rights of nationalities and minorities to freely pursue their culture, languages, traditions, etc. The Charter is satisfied with an individualistic, and even then a very weak, formulation in article 17(2) where it says 'Every individual may freely take part in the cultural life of his community'. This on a continent which is literally strewn with the so-called 'ethnic' conflicts and where some grievous violations of cultural etc., rights have taken place[27]. Yet, it may be emphasised again, these omissions are consistent with the practices of the states in Africa.

The Algerian Declaration stipulates the right to self-determination as 'imprescriptible and unalienable'. It also provides for the right to secession of a people from any 'colonial or foreign domination, whether direct or indirect, and from any racist regime', (arts. 5 and 6). So far, it seems the Declaration does not provide any thing more than the Charter although probably more strictly formulated. One of the limitations of the Declaration is precisely its reluctance to use fairly well-defined concepts such as 'nation' and 'nationality'. The question therefore is: Does the Declaration recognise the right of an oppressed nation (which is not a 'minority') within a sovereign state to secession? It seems not. This constitutes the greatest weakness of the Declaration and probably reflects the dominant tendency in Soviet 'socialism' and Eurocommunism. At the same time, the Algiers Declaration does provide for the right of a 'people' to speak its own language and develop its own culture, (art.13) including the right 'not to have an alien culture imposed upon it', (art.15). The cultural and language rights of minorities are also specifically recognised in article 19. Article 21 in this regard is interesting:

> These rights (of minorities) shall be exercised with due respect for the legitimate interests of the community as a whole and cannot authorise impairing the territorial integrity and political unity of the State, provided the State acts in accordance with all the principles set forth in this Declaration.

Presumably, therefore, a minority which is oppressed in any way could claim that the state concerned is not acting 'in accordance with all the principles set forth in this Declaration' and therefore it has a right to secede[28]. Thus, Cassese asserts, 'The bogey of secession has been exorcised'[29]. This may be true, but as I pointed out earlier, the Declaration is somewhat inconsistent and confused. While it recognises the right of an oppressed minority[30] to ultimate secession, it does not recognise the right of an oppressed nation to secede.

On the 'internal' right to self-determination, the Algiers Declaration exhibits great clarity and forthrightness. It links it with 'democratic government representing all citizens ... and capable of ensuring respect for the human rights and fundamental freedoms for all', (art.7). The formulation and spirit here is clearly anti-authoritarian. This contrasts sharply with the hesitant and ambiguous formulation (and probably the spirit too) of the African Charter. 'Every citizen shall have the right to participate freely in the government of his country, either directly or through freely chosen representatives in accordance with the provisions of the law'. At best, this provides for a representative government rather than a democratic one. And to add salt to the wound, the claw-back clause could enable any African government which has put the relevant law on the statute book and goes through the motions of electing representatives — as most of them do — to claim that they fulfil the requirements of this provision[31].

While still on self-determination, it is important to note that the African Charter raises the secondary elements in the principle of self-determination i.e. the questions of non-intervention and territorial integrity to the level of principal elements. It is not without irony that the OAU debate on Tanzania's invasion of Uganda on all sides was conducted on the level of the 'principle' of non-intervention and territorial integrity rather than that of self-determination. Thus President Nyerere justified his action in terms of self-defence and the territorial integrity of his country since Amin had first invaded Tanzania[32]. Clearly, this was a very weak argument once the Tanzanian troops went beyond repulsing the invading Amin troops and actually moved into Uganda up to the capital Kampala to 'liberate' it.

The principle of self-determination implies the right of the oppressed people to liberate themselves and not a foreign army doing it for them. Those who attacked Nyerere though never based their argument on the principle of self-determination either[33]. They actually defended Amin by arguing on the level of territorial integrity and non-intervention. This debate, and the ideological paradigms within which it was conducted, is a profound illustration of the truncated form in which the African states have appropriated the principle of self-determination and emasculated it of its anti-imperialist and democratic content.

Economic self-determination in the African Charter very closely follows the UN and UNCTAD-type tradition. It does not go further than the UN Resolution on Permanent Sovereignty over Natural Resources and backtracks even from that position by making that right (1) exercisable by states and (2) subjecting it 'to the obligation of promoting international economic co-operation based on mutual respect, equitable exchange and the principles of international law', (art.21)[34]. Laudable as these may sound, 'mutuality' and 'co-operation' in the typical African situation, where the economies are invariably dominated and exploited by foreign finance capital and multinationals, can, in practice, only mean an endorsement of the existing unequal, inequitable and exploitative imperialist relationships. This stands out in sharp relief when contrasted with the Algiers Declaration.

The 'fathers' of the Algiers Declaration were no doubt acutely aware of the colonial roots, including the plunder and spoliation that went with it, of the present underdevelopment in the Third World. Besides providing for the people's 'exclusive right over its natural wealth and resources' (art.8), the Declaration has some powerful provisions on the right to indemnity and restitution. The people have a right 'to recover them (i.e. natural wealth and resources)[35] if they have been despoiled, as well as any unjustly paid indemnities'. Under the section entitled 'Guarantees and Sanction', three articles provide further elucidation of the concept of unjust enrichment, historical and contemporary. These provisions deserve quotation:

> Article 24
>
> Any enrichment to the detriment of the people in violation of the provisions of this Declaration shall give rise to the restitution of profits thus obtained. The same shall be applied to all excessive profits on investments of foreign origin.
>
> Article 25
>
> Any unequal treaties, agreements or contracts concluded in disregard of the fundamental rights shall have no effect.
>
> Article 26
>
> External financial charges which become excessive and unbearable for the people shall cease to be due.

The neo-colonial character of the African Charter is even more starkly revealed in the resurrection of unbridled respect for private property. We have seen that this is a backward step compared to the UN Conventions. Even the European Convention does not contain it and it was included more or less as an afterthought in the First Protocol[36]. Even moderate African commentators have found it difficult to swallow it. Rembe suggests that one of the 'push-factors' for the inclusion of this right might have been to attract foreign aid and investments[37]. Indeed, what else! Rembe has further observed that this provision flies in the face of African states' oft-repeated obeisance to sovereignty over natural resources and the declarations of quite a few of them even to socialism. It blatantly negates the concepts of property even in African traditions and values which are supposed to have been the guiding light of the Charter. Rembe rightly points out the contradiction between the right to private property and the provisions on sovereignty over natural resources or eminent domain. Unlike Rembe, who seems to entertain some hope that a 'balance must be made between property ownership and eminent domain',[38] I do not see any such balance in the Charter or in the minds of the framers. Rather, taking into account the principles of international law to which the right to sovereignty over natural resources has been subordinated, it is clear that the right to private property has clearly come out on top. Who would be prepared to argue that that was not the intention of the 'founding fathers'?

The Algiers Declaration does not offer any protection to private property. A careful reading of its provisions shows that it is clearly aware that private property, in this case particularly imperialist property, lies behind the system of underdevelopment and domination in the Third World. Thus it partially[39] links the phenomenal level of unequal international exchange to its underlying basis in the exploitation of labour when it provides in article 10 that 'Every people has the right to a fair evaluation of its labour and to equal and just terms in international trade'. This, together with other provisions discussed before, negates totally the 'rights' of imperialist private property. And impliedly, I suggest, the Declaration subordinates the right to private property of nationals to the over-riding right of the people to, among other things, 'choose its own economic and social system and pursue its own path to economic development freely and without any foreign interference', (article 11).

RIGHT TO ORGANISE IN THE AFRICAN CHARTER AND THE ALGIERS DECLARATION

As would be expected by now, the right to organise receives a short shrift in the African Charter. 'Every individual shall have the right to free association provided he abides by the law', (art 10(1)). African state practice since independence abounds in 'laws' on the statute books which preach rights in the Preamble and pass over them in the enforceable body of the statute; which grant rights in the main clause and restrict them to negation in the provisos; as Marx said: '...liberty in a general phrase and its annihilation in the marginal note'[40]. The generality of the claw-back clause in the African Charter ensures that none of such laws on the statute books of its signatories offends the provisions of the Charter. Even worse, unlike the UN Conventions and the European and American Conventions, the African Charter does not specifically provide for the freedom to form and join trade unions[41]. This is obviously neither inadvertence of the draftsman nor simply a compromise among the signatories[42]. It is an accurate reflection of the almost universal practice of the member states of the OAU from Zaire to Algeria and from Senegal to Somalia. Whatever their public rhetoric and ideological persuasions, African ruling classes compensate for their economic weakness and political instability by denying their peoples the right to struggle and organise in opposition, protest and revolt.

The Algiers Declaration makes no bonds. It provides that 'Any people whose fundamental rights are seriously disregarded has the right to enforce them, especially by political or trade union struggle and even, in the last resort, by the use of force', (art. 28). This provision has a three-fold bias and shift of emphasis compared to the traditional formulation of, and spirit behind, the freedom of association. It sees the right to organise as a collective right of a social group (people) and not an individualistic right to associate; it is not restricted to the right to form only civil organisations but includes the right to form political organisations; it recognises that the right to organise extends up to and includes the right to the use of force i.e. the right to revolution, and finally it brings the concept of struggle for rights on the centre-stage as opposed to notions where rights are seen to be granted from above to the suppliant recipients. In all these respects, the African Charter's 'freedom of association' belongs to the opposite 'camp'. That brings us to, what the dominant discourse considers the lynchpin of a human rights convention, the machinery for enforcement of rights.

MACHINERY FOR ENFORCEMENT

Within its own conceptual framework and by the standards of international human rights regime, the African Charter is woefully deficient in its provisions on the machinery of enforcement. This has been commented upon by writers of differing standpoints[43]. The centrepiece is the African Commission consisting of eleven members who are elected by the OAU Assembly of the Heads of State from among the nominees of member states. While the Commissioners are supposed to serve in their personal capacity, it is interesting to note that the original Dakar Draft which specifically excluded 'a Government member or a member of the diplomatic corps' from occupying the office of the Commissioner involved a two-days debate at the end of which it was defeated[44]. Subsequent composition of the first Commission shows that, that defeat was very significant. All the eleven Commissioners elected were or still are occupants of important state positions in the apparatuses of their own governments[45]. It is trite to say that such Commissioners can hardly be expected to distance themselves from the anti-human rights practices or positions of their states. But then the Commission is not conceived of as a court with powers of impartial adjudication over alleged breaches of human rights.

The Commission receives communication from state party against another state. Ultimately, failing amicable solution (art.52), it reports back to the Assembly of the Heads of States and Governments. The

Commission may, if the majority so decides, receive and consider communications from elsewhere, presumably individuals and non-state organisations (art. 55(2)) provided the said communication satisfies the following conditions:

1. indicate their authors even if the latter request anonymity,
2. are compatible with the Charter of the Organization of African Unity or with the present Charter,
3. are not written in disparaging or insulting language directed against the State concerned and its institutions or to the Organization of African Unity,
4. are not based exclusively on news disseminated through the mass media,
5. are sent after exhausting local remedies, if any unless it is obvious that this procedure is unduly prolonged,
6. are submitted within a reasonable period from the time local remedies are exhausted or from the date the Commission is seized with the matter, and
7. do not deal with cases which have been settled by these States involved in accordance with the principles of the Charter of the United Nations, or the Charter of the Organization of African Unity or the provisions of the present Charter.

If the communication reveals any special case of massive violations, the Commission is to bring it to the notice of the Assembly of Heads of State and proceed for an in-depth study only if the Assembly so requests. Thus we are left with apparently cases of only individual or relatively minor violations. For the latter, the aforementioned conditions are formidable enough and probably meant to severely discourage communications from non-state sources. As a matter of fact, the Commission should immediately inform the State concerned of such a communication even before it is considered. Thus the anonymity provided for becomes spurious. In Africa, under such circumstances, one does not take risks of exposing oneself to the wrath of the offending state.

Finally, all reports, recommendations and results of the Commission's investigation are 'confidential until such a time as the Assembly of Heads of State and Government shall otherwise decide',(art.59(1)). One possible deterrent, publicity and exposure, is thus ruled out decisively. What then remains of the Commission? As it has been pointed out, it is no more than a subcommittee of the Assembly of the Heads of State, the very body which has hitherto maintained its, to use Nyerere's picturesque phraseology, 'solidarity of silence' on one another's misconduct. Not surprisingly, only Tanzania out of some more than 50 member states made bold to express its reservations on all articles associating the Commission to the Assembly of Heads of State and Government[46].

In keeping with its ideological thrust, the Algiers Declaration does not indulge in providing any machinery for the enforcement of rights. Rather it puts its faith in the people (and the international community of 'peoples', not states) to redress wrongs through their own organizations and, as a last resort, by the use of force. However, the Declaration does stipulate personal criminal and civil liability on those responsible for gross violations of fundamental rights of the peoples, (arts. 23 & 27). The strength of the Declaration lies not in providing any legalistic machinery, which, as the African Charter shows can be an empty shell devoid of much substance, but in generating international opinion on the one hand and legitimising the struggle and resistance of the people themselves against violations, on the other. This is the most that can be expected of a Declaration in the present conjuncture of international balance of forces.

The fact that the Algiers Declaration has received very little, if any, notice in the dominant human rights discourse on Africa testifies to the ideological biases of that discourse rooted in the hegemony of imperialist ideology. Human rights scholars of the dominant school take great pride in spilling a lot of ink on tinkering and refining the status quo rather than digging deep into its social and political character. They proclaim the universality of human rights concepts while ignoring the imperialist roots of their violations; they offer a set of institutions which supposedly signify democracy while pooh-poohing peoples' struggles in which democracy is rooted; they put the individual on the pedestal while the potential of the mass is crushed. Whence the responsibility of the intellectual?

NOTES

1. Francois Rigaux, 'The Algiers Declaration of the Rights of Peoples', in Cassese (ed.), *op.cit.*, pp.211-23 at p.211.
2. Jinadu, *op.cit.*, pp.42 *et seq.*
3. *Ibid.*, p.48; Falk, *op.cit.*, pp.226-7 and Chomsky & Herman, *op.cit.*, pp.33-4.
4. For an attempt by the EEC countries to include some mention of human rights in the Lome II Convention see Ronald I. Meltzer, 'International Human Rights and Development: Evolving Conceptions and Their Application to Relations between the European Community and the African-Caribbean-Pacific States', in Welch & Meltzer (eds.), *op.cit.*, pp.208-25 at pp.215-6.
5. Kannyo, 'Banjul Charter', *op.cit.*, p.142 and Olusola & Amadu, *op.cit.*

6. Quoted in Rembe, *op.cit.*, p.105.
7. Kannyo, 'Banjul Charter', *op.cit.*, p.145.
8. Rigaux, *op.cit.*, p.213. For an interesting discussion of progressive transnational NGOs, see A. Cassese 'Progressive Transnational Promotion of Human Rights' in B G Ramcheran, *Human Rights: Thirty Years after the Universal Declaration*. (The Hague: Martinus Nijhoft, 1979), p.249.
9. *Ibid.*, p.212.
10. *Ibid.*, p.213.
11. *Ibid.*, p.211.
12. For the practice of the OAU in this regard see Olusola & Amadu, *op.cit.*, pp.91-2.
13. In this respect the African Charter is a step backward compared to even the International Covenant on Economic, Social and Cultural Rights, 1966. Article 2(2) of the Covenant declares the freedom of all peoples to freely dispose of their natural wealth and resources 'without prejudice to any obligations arising out of ..., international law'. But Article 25, it can be argued, overrides any restrictions that may be imposed by customary international law, by stipulating in general terms that 'Nothing in this Covenant shall be interpreted as impairing the inherent right of all peoples to enjoy and utilize fully and freely their natural wealth and resources'. The African Charter, as is clear, has reversed the order and made the general right subject to international law.

    Not surprisingly, in his letters of submittal to President Carter (December 17, 1977), the US Deputy Secretary of State Warren Christopher had suggested a declaration with respect to the Covenant provisions discussed here to the effect that nothing in the Covenant derogates from 'the equal obligation of all States to fulfil their responsibilities under international law'. 'This declaration and understanding', the letter said, 'will make clear the United States position regarding property rights, and expresses the view of the United States that discrimination by developing countries against non-nationals or actions affecting their property or contractual rights may only be carried out in accordance with the governing rules of international law. Under international law, any taking of private property must be non-discriminatory and for a public purpose, and must be accompanied by prompt, adequate, and effective compensation'. Ironically, the African Charter comes very close to the US position! For the letter see The Department of State, *Selected Documents*, No.5, (Bureau of Public Affairs, Office of Public Communication), pp.49-58 at p.53.
14. For link between multinationals and human rights see Thomas E. McCarthy, 'Transnational Corporations and Human Rights', Cassese (ed.), *op.cit.*, pp.175-95.
15. Rigaux, *op.cit.*, p.219.
16. Algiers Declaration, Rigaux, *op.cit.*, p.219.
17. See the Preamble, clause 3.
18. *Ibid.*, clause 8. Interestingly the original Dakar Draft did not have this terminology. And the inclusion of 'zionism' in the text seems to have been by default rather than a conscious ideological act. See Richard Gittleman, 'The Banjul Charter on Human and People's Rights: A Legal Analysis', in Welch & Meltzer, *op.cit.*, pp.152-76 at fns. 10 & 11.
19. See above, p.83 et seq.
20. For the social and material basis of these positions see Issa G. Shivji, 'OAU: Some Reflections', in Peter A. Nyong'o, *Africa between Capitalist Crisis and Socialist Transformation* (Trenton: Africa World Press, forthcoming).
21. For Toure's deplorable human rights record see AI: *Briefing on Guinea* (London: June, 1978). See also Lansine Kaba, 'The Cultural Revolution, Artistic Creativity and Freedom of Expression in Guinea', *Journal of Modern African Studies* 14, no.2 (1976), pp.201-18.

22. Quoted in Kannyo, 'Banjul Charter', *op.cit.*, p.146.
23. The 1948 one is a little more elaborate on 'duty'. Both reproduced in Brownlie, *Human Rights, op.cit.*, pp. 381 & 391.
24. For the discussion of the concept of 'duty' in the African Charter see Gittleman, *op.cit.*, p.154.
25. Quoted in Olusola & Amadu, *op.cit.*, pp. 93-3.
26. *Ibid.*, p.6.
27. Neff, *op.cit.*, p.9.
28. See Cassese, *op.cit.*, for this interpretation.
29. *Ibid.*, p.155.
30. As I have already pointed out, the use of the term 'minority' in the Declaration without at the same time the use of the concepts of 'nation' and 'nationality' probably partly account for this confusion. The term 'minority' is widely used in international instruments and traces its origin to various 'minority' treaties entered into by the European powers after the first world war. Cf. Rodolfo de Nova, 'The International Protection of National Minorities and Human Rights', *Howard Law Journal* 11, no. 2 (Spring, 1965), pp.275-90.
31. See Neff, *ibid.*
32. Kannyo, 'Banjul Charter', *op.cit.*, p.146.
33. The hegemony of the statist interpretation of the principle of self-determination is further evidenced by the fact that even among intellectual and progressive circles in East Africa the debate on the so-called 'liberation' of Uganda was never conducted within the Leninist parameters of self-determination.
34. See discussion above, p.96.
35. To be sure, the Charter has one obscure provision which says 'In case of spoliation the dispossessed people shall have the right to the *lawful* recovery of its property as well as to an adequate compensation'. The use of the term 'lawful' is worrisome; it probably means in accordance with the provisions of international law in which case the apparent progressive content of the article is nullified.
36. Rembe, *op.cit.*, p.117.
37. *Ibid.*, p.220, fn. 31. (The printing of footnotes in this book is badly done as the order of the footnotes to chapters three and four is reversed.)
38. *Ibid.*, p.117.
39. Partially because the Declaration, correctly in my opinion, is framed within a general anti-imperialist, democratic framework and not a socialist one.
40. Quoted in Szabo, *Socialist Concept, op.cit.*, p. 40.
41. See Neff, *op.cit.*, pp.6-7.
42. Generally on the right to form NGOs etc. see Scoble, 'Human Rights Non-Governmental Organizations', *op.cit.*
43. See, *inter alia*, P. K. A.Amoah, 'The African Charter on Human and People's Rights: Implementation Machinery', Gaborone Seminar, *op.cit.*; Gittleman, *op.cit.*, Olusanya and Amadu, *op.cit.*, Rembe, *op.cit.*
44. Gittleman, *op.cit.*, p.174, fn.56.
45. See the OAU Document AHG/146 (XXIII) which gives the curriculum vitae of the candidates for the post of commissioners.
46. Rembe, *op.cit.*, p.114.

CONCLUSION: AN AGENDA FOR RESEARCH

Several issues and areas have been thrown up by this work which have been either under-researched or very often unresearched. As we observed before, the human rights discourse in and on Africa lags behind that in other social sciences. Therefore, among the first research tasks, is to bring the human rights discourse within the fold of social science debate as at the same time to bring the advances made in the social sciences to bear upon that discourse. This very critique needs to be discussed and debated as part of an agenda for research.

Secondly, while there are general works on imperialism in Africa, there is a dearth of concrete studies which document and reveal the 'doings' of imperialism on the continent. This calls for a serious study of empirical material and its documentation. It should indeed include the role of the US, West European powers as well as the Soviet Union and the East European countries. Such work cannot be left to Africanists or to cold war propagandists. African scholars and intellectuals should bring their commitment to bear upon this subject on the continental level.

Thirdly, the rights that we have suggested as the central rights — the 'right to self-determination' and the 'right to organise' — are undertheorised in their practical and historical application to Africa. This again is a very important area of further work taking into account the real struggles of the people and the way these rights manifest themselves in practical life. Coupled with that would go the further deepening and broadening of the concepts of 'nation', 'nationality', 'people' etc. Conflicts in Africa are still predominantly interpreted in colonial-anthropological framework of 'tribal', ethnic or racial conflicts[1]. While some of the concepts mentioned may not be directly applicable, they would be sharpened in the very process of application taking into account the historical specificity of the African continent.

Fourthly, the theorisation of 'state' also remains inadequate. True, it has received greater attention in the social sciences; yet even this work has not been utilised sufficiently in the human rights discourse.

Fifthly, closely connected with the question of the state is the question of law and legal ideology. The formalistic positivism of African lawyers has meant that there is practically very little which can be seriously described as African jurisprudence. African lawyers have rarely ventured beyond rules and statutes or, if they have, they have tended to regurgitate the Kelsens and the Dworkins. Thus the whole arena of jurisprudence has been left to American academics in African universities to expound their 'law and development' theology.

Yet the whole question of the African jurisprudence as it has developed over the last three decades of independence on the one hand, and the hegemony or otherwise of legal ideology among the large mass of the people on the other, require immediate attention[2].

As I have emphasised repeatedly in this study, human rights should be seen in the wider context of the struggles of the African people. Therefore, there is a need to dovetail research programmes in human rights into those dealing with social and political movements. Both these areas should be able to focus on the varied forms of resistance and struggle of the people; draw lessons from them and theorise explanations for failures and successes.

Human rights research, needless to say, should not be isolated from the practical work of exposing massive violations of rights on our continent. It is shameful that African intellectuals should have singularly failed to form serious continental and countrywide organisations to deal with human rights questions concretely. It is even more shameful when such organisations, when formed, become simply means of soliciting and receiving foreign funding. Fund-hunting becomes their principal activity to the exclusion of grass-root work. Continental and other human rights organisations should seriously try to root themselves in the local environment with local material support.

Without the understanding of all these areas, human rights discourse and activity will continue to grope in the dark, mindlessly reproducing imperialist and neo-colonial ideological domination.

NOTES

1. The concepts of 'nation' and 'nationality' are used very little and so is the principle of self-determination. I came across only one work along these lines in the human rights discourse. See Humphrey Nwosu, 'The Concepts of Nationalism and Right to Self-determination: Cameroon as a Case Study', *Africa Quarterly* 16, no.2:1-26 (October, 1976).
2. For some thoughts on this see Issa G. Shivji, 'Law in Independent Africa: Some Reflections on the Role of Legal Ideology', *Ohio State Law Journal* 46, no.3, pp.689-96.

APPENDIX

UNIVERSAL DECLARATION OF THE RIGHTS OF PEOPLES (ALGIERS, 4 JULY 1976)

Preamble

We live at a time of great hopes and deep despair; a time of conflicts and contradictions; a time when liberation struggles have succeeded in arousing the peoples of the world against the domestic and international structures of imperialism and in overturning colonial systems; a time of struggle and victory in which new ideals of justice among and within nations have been adopted; a time when the General Assembly of the United Nations has given increasing expression, from the Universal Declaration of Human Rights to the Charter on the Economic Rights and Duties of States, to the quest for a new international, political and economic order.

But this is also a time of frustration and defeat, as new forms of imperialism evolve to oppress and exploit the peoples of the world. Imperialism, using vicious methods, with the complicity of governments that it has itself often installed, continues to dominate a part of the world. Through direct or indirect intervention, through multinational enterprises, through manipulation of corrupt local politicians, with the assistance of military regimes based on police repression, torture and physical extermination of opponents, through a set of practices that has become known as neo-colonialism, imperialism extends its stranglehold over many peoples.

Aware of expressing the aspirations of our era, we met in Algiers to proclaim that all the peoples of the world have an equal right to liberty, the right to free themselves from any foreign interference and to choose their own government, the right if they are under subjection, to fight for their liberation and the right to benefit from other peoples' assistance in their struggle.

Convinced that the effective respect for human rights necessarily implies respect for the rights of peoples, we have adopted the Universal Declaration for the Rights of Peoples.

May all those who, throughout the world, are fighting the great battle, at times through armed struggle, for the freedom of all peoples, find in this Declaration the assurance of the legitimacy of their struggle.

Section I. Right to Existence

Article 1
Every people has the right to existence.

Article 2
Every people has the right to the respect of its national and cultural identity.

Article 3
Every people has the right to retain peaceful possession of its territory and to return to it if it is expelled.

Article 4
None shall be subjected, because of his national or cultural identity, to massacre, torture, persecution, deportation, expulsion or living conditions such as may compromise the identity or integrity of the people to which he belongs.

Section II Right to Political Self-determination

Article 5
Every people has an imprescriptible and unalienable right to self-determination. It shall determine its political status freely and without any foreign interference.

Article 6
Every people has the right to break free from any colonial or foreign domination, whether direct or indirect, and from any racist regime.

Article 7
Every people has the right to have democratic government representing all the citizens without distinction as to race, sex, belief or colour, and capable of ensuring effective respect for the human rights and fundamental freedoms for all.

Section III. Economic Rights of Peoples

Article 8
Every people has an exclusive right over its natural wealth and

resources. It has the right to recover them if they have been despoiled, as well as any unjustly paid indemnities.

Article 9
Scientific and technical progress being part of the common heritage of mankind, every people has the right to participate in it.

Article 10
Every people has the right to a fair evaluation of its labour and to equal and just terms in international trade.

Article 11
Every people has the right to choose its own economic and social system and pursue its own path to economic development freely and without any foreign interference.

Article 12
The economic rights set forth shall be exercised in a spirit of solidarity amongst the peoples of the world and with due regard for their respective interests.

Section IV. Right to Culture

Article 13
Every people has the right to speak its own language and preserve and develop its own culture, thereby contributing to the enrichment of the culture of mankind.

Article 14
Every people has the right to its artistic, historical and cultural wealth.

Article 15
Every people has the right not to have an alien culture imposed upon it.

Section V. Right to Environment and Common Resources

Article 16
Every people has the right to the conservation, protection and improvement of its environment.

Article 17
Every people has the right to make use of the common heritage of mankind, such as the high seas, the sea-bed, and outer space.

Article 18

In the exercise of the preceding rights every people shall take account of the necessity for coordinating the requirements of its economic development with solidarity amongst all the peoples of the world.

Section VI. Rights of Minorities

Article 19

When a people constitutes a minority within a State it has the right to respect for its identity, traditions, language and cultural heritage.

Article 20

The members of a minority shall enjoy without discrimination the same rights as the other citizens of the State and shall participate on an equal footing with them in public life.

Article 21

These rights shall be exercised with due respect for the legitimate interests of the community as a whole and cannot authorise impairing the territorial integrity and political unity of the State, provided the State acts in accordance with all the principles set forth in this Declaration.

Section VII. Guarantees and Sanctions

Article 22

Any disregard for the provisions of this Declaration constitutes a breach of obligations towards the international community as a whole.

Article 23

Any prejudice resulting from disregard for this Declaration must be totally compensated by whoever caused it.

Article 24

Any enrichment to the detriment of the people in violation of the provisions of this Declaration shall give rise to the restitution of profits thus obtained. The same shall be applied to all excessive profits on investments of foreign origin.

Article 25

Any unequal treaties, agreements or contracts concluded in disregard of the fundamental rights or peoples shall have no effect.

Article 26
External financial charges which become excessive and unbearable for the people shall cease to be due.

Article 27
The gravest violations of the fundamental rights of peoples, especially of their right to existence, constitute international crimes for which their perpetrators shall carry personal penal liability.

Article 28
Any people whose fundamental rights are seriously disregarded has the right to enforce them, specially by political or trade union struggle and even, in the last resort by the use of force.

Article 29
Liberation movements shall have access to international organisations and their combatants are entitled to the protection of the humanitarian law of war.

Article 30
The re-establishment of the fundamental rights of peoples, when they are seriously disregarded, is a duty incumbent upon all members of the international community.

INDEX

B

C

CPSIA information can be obtained
at www.ICGtesting.com
Printed in the USA
LVHW031748171220
674449LV00003B/628